A COLLABORATIVE APPROACH TO CREATING
MEANINGFUL IDENTITIES

Designing Brands

gestalten   BY GESTALTEN & CREATIVE VOYAGE

Table of Contents

Introduction

When Studio8585, one of the eight studios featured throughout *Designing Brands* and the design consultancy responsible for Creative Voyage, the educational platform behind the book, turned 10 years old, we wanted to celebrate it. Our team sat down, and we discussed how we got here. After significant back and forth, it became very apparent that the studio's success owes a whole lot to its collaborators—the brands it partners with, the other designers and teams that serve as constant inspiration, and the photographers, illustrators, animators, strategists, writers, and web developers who help execute its visions. How boring, we then thought, to create a book focused squarely on Studio8585's work.

As with many firms, Studio8585 revels in brand identity development. It is an honor to bring the visual worlds of these like-minded ventures to life. In that sense, *Designing Brands* is a love letter to this discipline. The book is not a detailed how-to guide but a testament to some of the most beautiful, exciting identities that we see today and the people behind them. We explore brands—a small-batch Australian whiskey distiller, a Norwegian LGBTQIA+ health organization, and a global design retailer, among others—that vary in size, industry, reach, and location. We gather a group of studios and industry experts to share their experiences and their guiding principles. Yet, we keep the conversation open. *Designing Brands* isn't prescriptive; it is a focused and hopefully inspiring resource for designers of today—and tomorrow. It is as much about the important questions as it is the answers.

The identity creation process, it seems, is far from linear. As with most creative pursuits, there are a series of necessary phases, but it is impossible to completely streamline the steps. The progression is ever-evolving, and there are no set rules or regulations. As such, we approach this practice by breaking it down into eight elements that define our chapters: discovery, direction, typography, illustration, photography, design, digital, and physical. We have deemed these the essential ingredients—as described at the start of each section by Mario Depicolzuane, founder of both Studio8585 and Creative Voyage—for a well-crafted brand universe. And to back us up, we called on seven other design firms across the globe.

We chose these studios for their holistic portfolios, for their shared values—timelessness and thoughtfulness at their core—and for their considered collection of collaborators. Again, this is a community effort, and we wanted to ensure that was reflected across the board. These ateliers, all of whom we have immense admiration for, are woven throughout the book's figurative fabric. We hope that the result feels like a thought-provoking discussion between these designers, the specialists that we have selected to exemplify each element, and our readers.

Nearly every person who offers their thoughts in these pages speaks to the value of emotional connection. A brand, they say, is more than an exceptional logo, typography suite, or website. Rather, a brand is defined by how these components come together to communicate something larger. "Products are created in a factory, but brands are created in the mind," remarked the German-born branding and consumer research pioneer Walter Landor. Designers are responsible for providing brands the tools to become living, breathing entities that break through the noise and interact with their intended audiences. They can shift and evolve, and should have a visual architecture that supports their slow, inevitable transformations. People, after all, fall in love with brands, developing a sense of trust, loyalty, and satisfaction. Much like real-life relationships, those between brands and consumers can be short or long. They can be based on lust and attraction, companionship, or mere functionality.

Without designers and their peers, from the typographic wizard to the print-production prodigy, a brand struggles to convert its thoughts and feelings into action. These creatives take on enormous but often behind-the-scenes roles. In *Designing Brands*, we're bringing them center stage—not because they're crying for attention, but because in order to see more great work in an ever-changing, highly saturated landscape, we have to call out the quiet minds that are creating with intentionality, patience, consistency, and dedication. At Creative Voyage, we champion these voices. This book is an ode to the design agencies and the many other contributors behind the brands with whom we have developed our own deeply meaningful ties.

A brand is greater than the sum of its parts. But to best understand how a well-rounded identity is born, we have divided *Designing Brands* into eight chapters based on the most critical of components. The elements, as we call them, will guide you through the journey from mood board to established brand universe.

I Discovery

II Direction

III Typography

IV Illustration

Laying the groundwork for ideation by diving deep into a brand's world and reference materials

Applying research and data to make the master plan and carve a path forward

Arranging letters and text and choosing typefaces to tether a brand to its message

Filling the gaps where words lack power with pictorial symbols and graphic icons

PROJECTS

Atelier Dyakova: Paper Foundation
1/1 Studio: J. Hannah

PROJECTS

Bielke&Yang: Sommerro
TRiC: Hillwood

PROJECTS

Sascha Lobe: The Conran Shop
Atelier Dyakova: Mad et Len

PROJECTS

Bielke&Yang: Helseutvalget
Studio FNT: Onharu

V   Photography

Producing and directing still and
moving images to breathe life into
a brand's narratives

VI   Design

Unifying graphic elements—layouts,
grids, logos, and more—to create an
architecture that lasts

VII   Digital

Bringing brands into the modern day
with websites, mobile applications,
and online experiences

VIII   Physical

Creating real-life, tangible
collateral, from printed matter
to in-person activations

These eight influential studios from around the globe are the guiding lights throughout *Designing Brands*. In conversation and through some of their most successful projects to date, they share their methods and philosophies, drawing back the curtain on the profound process that is brand identity development.

Sascha Lobe / Pentagram

The German designer Sascha Lobe joined the illustrious graphics firm Pentagram as a partner in 2018. He has since assembled a robust team in London, where his ever-growing, extensive portfolio continues to blossom.

SELECTED CLIENTS

Adidas
Amorepacific
Cocorico
Mercedes-Benz
Vitra

Mouthwash Studio

Born in 2019 as the brainchild of Abraham Campillo, Alex Tan, Mackenzie Freemire, and Ben Mingo, Mouthwash Studio is a multidisciplinary design agency in Los Angeles that relies on experimentation and intuition at its core.

SELECTED CLIENTS

Blind Barber
Cosmos
Nike Run Club
Post Company
Rose Los Angeles

Studio8585

Established in 2013, Studio8585 is a creative practice helmed by founder Mario Depicolzuane and Benja Pavlin. Despite an official base in Zagreb, Croatia, the studio's de facto office exists wherever the members of its small team currently hang their hats.

SELECTED CLIENTS

Audo Copenhagen
Design Hotels
Kinfolk
Harvard GSD
Space10

Atelier Dyakova

Atelier Dyakova has built a firm foundation in conceptual and typographic experimentation since 2014. Located in London, the creative consultancy is led by Sonya Dyakova, who originally hails from Siberian Russia.

SELECTED CLIENTS

David Zwirner
Frieze
Gerbase
The Wapping Project
Lemaire

TRiC

Founded by Tristan Ceddia and Rick Milovanovic, TRiC specializes in strategic design thinking. Since its inception in 2020, this Melbourne-based studio has been carefully amassing a roster of conscientious clients and collaborators.

SELECTED CLIENTS

Hagen's
Lagoon Dining
Office MI—JI
Q Le Baker
Tamsin Johnson

Bielke&Yang

Formed in 2012 by Christian Bielke and Martin Yang, the Oslo-based studio Bielke&Yang produces simple, functional design solutions that are at once deeply Norwegian and international in aesthetic.

SELECTED CLIENTS

A. Huseby
E24
Klar
P. A. Larsen
Talormade

Studio FNT

Brought to life in 2006 by Jaemin Lee, Heesun Kim, and Woogyung Geel, Seoul-based Studio FNT is a full-service agency bringing a fresh perspective to the Korean design scene with its grounded and timeless techniques.

SELECTED CLIENTS

Felt
The Hyundai Seoul
Kara
Space K
University of Seoul

1/1 Studio

1/1 Studio, the Auckland atelier headed up by Natasha Sawicki Mead and Joe Swann since 2017, partners with progressive fashion, art, and lifestyle brands across the globe that share their tactile, nuanced, and purposeful approach.

SELECTED CLIENTS

Are Studio
Everyday Needs
LoQ
Shaina Mote
Sans [ceuticals]

Studios work side by side with external partners to realize their plans. At its heart, *Designing Brands* is about relationships—the close-knit community of creative directors, strategists, manufacturers, illustrators, stylists, photographers, and tastemakers who unite in service of a brand's visual world. These eight expert voices offer a more in-depth look into these collaborations.

Amanda Gunawan & Joel Wong

Amanda Gunawan and Joel Wong formed their Los Angeles-based architecture and design studio OWIU in 2017. Working in concert is central to Gunawan and Wong's approach, both when serving clients and acting as clients themselves.

SELECTED CLIENTS

For the Win
Goho Kaiseki & Bar
Henry Golding and Liv Lo
Mezcla
Ms. Maria & Mr. Singh

Hector Muelas

With a penchant for everything identity, the globe-trotting creative director Hector Muelas has put his stamp on iconic brands from Rimowa to Apple and DKNY since the onset of the new millennium.

SELECTED CLIENTS

Coca-Cola
LVMH
Madhappy
Vice
Wheely

Dinamo

Established in 2013 by Johannes Breyer and Fabian Harb, Dinamo is a type foundry that has positioned itself as an innovator in its field, offering everything from design software to research services and, of course, typefaces.

SELECTED CLIENTS

Acqua di Parma
MIT
Bauhaus 100
International Olympic Committee
Yale Architecture Press

Mario Hugo

Since co-founding the New York-based artist management agency Hugo & Marie in 2008, the illustrator and designer Mario Hugo has served as a guidepost for creative pursuits and collaborative identity development.

SELECTED CLIENTS

Atmos
Equinox Hotels
Hourglass
The Row
Saint Laurent

Alexander Saladrigas

A proud product of Miami now stationed in New York, the photographer Alexander Saladrigas continues to garner a wide range of clients with his humanistic gaze and body of work marked by soft textures and a rich color palette.

SELECTED CLIENTS

Carolina Herrera
Christopher John Rogers
Giorgio Armani
Kate Spade
Opening Theory

Astrid Stavro

Italian designer Astrid Stavro has built a global sphere of influence from Atlas, the design consultancy she co-founded in 2013, to Pentagram, where she served as partner, and Collins, where she holds court as VP, Creative Director.

SELECTED CLIENTS

Camper
Fedrigoni
The National Portrait Gallery
Phaidon
Reina Sofía Museum

Zhenya Rynzhuk

The Ukrainian digital designer Zhenya Rynzhuk hit the ground running when she co-founded Synchronized Studio in 2016. Her avant-garde and nomadic atelier has garnered recognition thanks to its trailblazing approach to crafting digital worlds.

SELECTED CLIENTS

Adobe
Visual Creatures
Google
Forner
Spacelab

Imprimerie du Marais

In the realm of printing, Imprimerie du Marais knows little competition. Since 1971, the many-faceted Parisian family business has tackled highly ambitious commissions from some of the world's most coveted brands.

SELECTED CLIENTS

Acne Studios
Balmain
L:a Bruket
Lanvin
The Macallan

I

Discovery

The Art of Strategy

Research
& Exploration

As the businessman, leadership expert, and writer Stephen R. Covey once observed, "You don't have much confidence in someone who doesn't diagnose before they prescribe." The diagnosis process, often referred to as "discovery," comprises the first essential phase in developing a meaningful brand identity. This journey begins with an inquiry, frequently casual and sometimes well-articulated. It can come in the form of a conversation, a text, an email, a written brief from a client, or even a thoughtfully designed deck. As brand strategists and designers, we need to understand as best we can the context—the scope, purpose, and intended audience, but also execution ideas, mood references, and other expectations—of the project at hand.

This first step lays the foundation for the entire design process. Through meetings, calls, or multi-day workshops, designers and clients work closely together to gain a deep understanding of the brand and its target audience. The goal is to create an identity that resonates and effectively communicates the brand's values and personality. In the informative book *Art Direction Explained, At Last!* designer and D&AD executive committee member Vince Frost put it aptly: "Don't talk over your clients or your workmates. The clues are everywhere." In other words, we start as though we don't know a thing. We prompt conversation by asking questions, but we don't assert opinions or solutions just yet. It can be easy to jump in with our creative impulse. The first solution we envision might be the right one, but without proper due diligence, it's impossible to know.

Our best tools can be curiosity and strategic inquiry. We need to learn the brand's history, vision, and mission. And to create an identity that truly reflects its essence, we, too, need to understand their competition, demographics, and market position. The answers lie in research. Crafting a simple questionnaire or survey can prove the best way to start these requisite conversations. What are the client's deepest beliefs and values (or as the brand consultant and author Andy Green once suggested, the "things [they] do even when it hurts")? At their core, who are they? What makes their brand distinctive? Ask the serious questions, but also ask the fun questions. What is the client watching, reading, or listening to? If the brand was a movie character, who would it be?

We gather as much information as we can. We conduct a visual audit, making our way through the brand's existing identity, and explore references that align accordingly. We distill our findings into a mission statement of sorts—a tagline or even a full-fledged manifesto—that describes the brand's unique premise. As graphic design expert and author of *Branding: In Five and a Half Steps* Michael Johnson explains, this statement provides an answer to the question of all questions: "Why are we here?" Once we have our resolution— and in close collaboration with the client—we can develop a brand strategy that outlines its overall vision, defines its key attributes, and sets the tone for its future messaging.

The final step of this phase is developing a thorough understanding of the assignment itself, which we often articulate and share with the client in the form of a creative brief. This document describes the project's scope, objectives, and target audience. It lays out the initial creative direction, design requirements, and timelines. In essence, it is our roadmap. The creative brief ensures that everyone involved is aligned, working towards the same goals, and following a consistent and coherent direction. Keep in mind: this is a living document, and it can shift and mature. We can't forget to leave room for serendipity and instinct.

Discovery is an art of its own. Though we all develop our own tactics, this process is crucial for each and every studio. While it can vary from project to project, it is nevertheless the key to successful work—even when it comes to the simplest of assignments. After all, this period of examination leads to more than tangible goals. It also provides an opportunity to earn client trust and respect, grounding tools that are the cornerstones of not just brand development but maintenance and evolution, too.

Amanda Gunawan & Joel Wong

*Keeping Up
with the Clients*

The Biscuit Loft, an apartment housed within the former Nabisco cookie factory and redesigned by the OWIU team, houses the company headquarters and serves as a physical manifestation of the brand's values.

The Los Angeles-based architecture and design firm OWIU has a longer name and one that is really more of a motto. "The only way is up," its co-founders Amanda Gunawan and Joel Wong say, "is a lifestyle." The expression that has woven its way into their studio, their home, and their everyday lives implies an always upward trajectory and a constant state of evolution. It makes sense, then, that after starting their firm in 2017, they found themselves looking to rebrand.

Much like their work, Gunawan and Wong's ascent has been simultaneously progressive and mindful. Both raised in Singapore, the duo met in high school. They then studied at the Southern California Institute of Architecture before joining Morphosis, the interdisciplinary practice from Pritzker Prize-winner Thom Mayne. After just under one year working at the prestigious office, they received an email from Paris Design Week asking if they wanted to exhibit furniture that they had produced while students. Gunawan and Wong found themselves at a turning point, but true to their slogan, they kept forging ahead. They subsequently left their coveted jobs at Morphosis behind and set OWIU right into motion. Fast-forward, and they

2

When Gunawan and Wong launched OWIU Goods, a homewares line focused on ceramic objects, they sought the help of Studio8585 to develop an identity, which ultimately led to an entire company rebrand.

3

have developed not just one business but four—OWIU Goods, OWIU Design, Inflexion Builds, and OWIU Spaces. They were due for a refresh. "We felt like we had outgrown our identity," say Gunawan and Wong. "OWIU had become so much more than what it was at the start. We wanted something that could reflect that shift."

As with many things in life, landing on the right design studio wasn't straightforward. In fact, Gunawan and Wong didn't find their eventual collaborator Mario Depicolzuane at all—rather, he discovered them. They clicked after he asked Gunawan to contribute to a newsletter for his educational platform Creative Voyage. Shortly thereafter, she enlisted his design firm Studio8585 for a smaller project: crafting an identity for their new homewares line OWIU Goods.

Gunawan and Wong's own experience working closely with others to transform their needs and visions into remarkable spaces meant that they were well-equipped to jump into this process with ease. In their own projects, they begin the discovery phase by asking clients to compose a mood board. "This exercise forces them to pick and choose what they like," Gunawan and Wong assert. "And from there, we are able to predict what they gravitate towards and understand their sense of style." They liken their approach to therapy, where empathy is imperative. For Depicolzuane to work on any arm of the business, he needed a firm grasp on their entire model. "We were very thorough when it came to explaining our processes," Gunawan and Wong recall. They were so thorough, in fact, that as Depicolzuane was finalizing the branding for OWIU Goods, they realized that he was the man for their identity-at-large.

"It came down to talent, of course, but also working and communication style," Gunawan and Wong say of their intuitive decision to continue their collaboration with Depicolzuane's atelier. The duo maintained contact with the Studio8585 team on email but more regularly, on WhatsApp. This platform allowed for intimate and immediate interactions, which complement active movers and shakers like Gunawan and Wong. They constantly exchanged inspiration material such as architecture practices, notes from their travels, interesting manufacturers in Japan, as well as notes on other successful companies like NYC perfume label Le Labo.

The cult-favorite skincare brand Aesop became another primary reference. "They built a company with values and qualities that we wanted to emulate," say Gunawan and Wong. "They made clean, simple everyday products iconic and prestigious." The OWIU partners also admired the level of craftsmanship in Aesop's branding combined with its ability to transform each of its stores into an inimitable retail experience. "We let concepts like these marinate," the OWIU founders explain. "We explored a lot of different angles and routes, seeking a forward-thinking aesthetic solution but not anything overly novel."

Together with Depicolzuane and the Studio8585 team, Gunawan and Wong pieced together key elements from a wide range of resources to develop an identity uniquely their own. Each branch of the business has a distinct design language with elements, such as a typographic approach, that tie them together. Like the very things that OWIU creates, whether interior spaces or glazed ceramics, its identity is one that exudes thoughtfulness, timelessness, and care. Given their audience, which ranges from couples and families to restaurateurs and developers, the multifaceted company sought a sense of clarity. The subtle design applications resonate most with Gunawan and Wong, but the art direction of imagery, the selected typeface, and the overall online experience capture the brand narrative, allowing them to better interact with potential customers or clients.

For Studio8585 and OWIU, a mutual respect for each other's work gave way to a peer-to-peer relationship that made the final result all the more powerful. With an openness to express ideas and opinions, they found a solution that both sides are proud of. Gunawan and Wong believe that, when choosing to work with a design firm, it's vital to place significant faith and trust in them. "At the same time," they say, "the designer can never be complacent." When the only way is up, they continue, "the design process should be progressive, always looking to improve iteration by iteration." And so the branding process is far from over. The WhatsApp thread with Depicolzuane continues, and bit by bit, the OWIU identity takes a different shape.

4

5

2 — HANDMADE CERAMIC BOWL FOR OWIU GOODS
3 — SMALL-BATCH PIECES FROM LOCAL EARTH
4 — RYOKAN-STYLE REDESIGN OF A LOS ANGELES HOME
5 — ARCHITECTURE AND DESIGN FOR RAPPU HANDROLL BAR

LONDON-BASED DESIGNER SASCHA LOBE
IS A PARTNER AT PENTAGRAM

Sascha Lobe/Pentagram

Sascha Lobe is a man of many talents. Before landing on graphic design, he dove into electrical engineering, following his interests in math and physics. Then, he turned towards architecture, considering a career in the field before he grew concerned with its slow pace of output. Finally, he found his calling: a discipline that merged a science-like attention to detail with free-flowing creativity. After running his own Stuttgart-based firm, L2M3, for nearly 20 years, Lobe received a formal invitation from the iconic Paula Scher. "Could you ever imagine becoming a Pentagram partner?" she asked. He said yes, and since 2018, the German designer has been further cementing his reputation as one of the finest in his field.

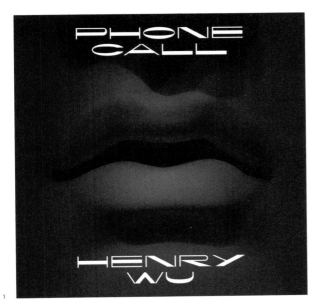

1

2

What does a brand stand to gain from working with a partner at Pentagram, the world's largest independent design consultancy? From a designer's point of view, Pentagram feels quite similar to a small studio. It is composed of 22 partners who manage their own projects and team. The advantage of being part of Pentagram is that we can draw upon our collective legacy, experience, and resources, which allows us to provide the expertise and capabilities of a larger design agency. Put simply, Pentagram combines the best of both worlds: the qualities of a boutique studio and the capabilities of a Madison Avenue agency. We have the agility and personalized approach of the former, allowing us to provide individualized attention to each client and project. At the same time, we possess the assets, expertise, and reputation that rival those of the big players. This unique blend sets Pentagram apart and makes it one of the most exceptional design firms I have ever come across. It's a concept that, in my opinion, is unparalleled. The level of creativity, craftsmanship, and strategic thinking that exists within our organization is truly remarkable.

How does your passion for architecture impact your work? I have a deep passion for various disciplines from art to design, fashion, and music. These interests fuel my creativity and inspire me to explore the intersections between different mediums. The principles of the Bauhaus movement and the concept of a Gesamtkunstwerk, which encompasses the synthesis of different art forms, are core to my approach. For me, the boundaries between 2D and 3D are fluid, and I effortlessly navigate between graphic ideas and spatial expressions. I find joy in seamlessly blending these elements and shaping harmonious experiences.

I have an insatiable curiosity when it comes to embarking on new projects and exploring uncharted territories, which is how I grow both personally and professionally. Yet I firmly believe that the key to success lies in collaborating with the right people. One of my most valuable partnerships is with the brand strategist and creative director Kimberly Lloyd. Her expansive knowledge, strategic thinking, and keen sense of taste have greatly expanded my horizons. Together, we have achieved outstanding results that I couldn't have accomplished on my own. While my natural inclination leans towards simplicity and minimalism, often influenced by my background in architecture, I am aware that this approach may have limitations when it comes to building brands with broad appeal. That is where Kimberly steps in, bridging

1 — IDENTITY FOR "PHONE CALL" SINGLE FROM HENRY WU, ALSO KNOWN AS KAMAAL WILLIAMS
2 — VISUAL ASSETS FOR KAMAAL WILLIAMS'S *STINGS* LP

from abc to cd
the visual identity
of the bauhaus-archiv
berlin

sascha lobe, L2M3
centre pompidou
17th of june, 7pm

the gap and ensuring that our projects have the necessary depth, reach, and impact. As a result, we develop identities that are both visually astonishing and capable of resonating with diverse audiences.

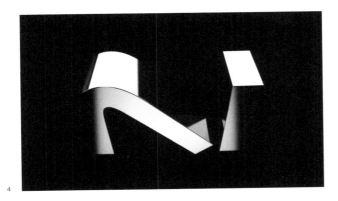

Speaking of curiosity, what role does teaching play in your career? A few years after graduating from art school, I dove into teaching. It turned out to be a transformative experience, one that pushed me to articulate my ideas and concepts with words and gain a deeper understanding of my own desires, preferences, and aspirations. For over a decade, I dedicated myself to being a professor, sharing my knowledge and nurturing the creative minds of my students. It was a rewarding journey, but as time passed, I began to sense repetition in the cycle. Last year, I made the decision to temporarily step away from teaching, recognizing that I had come full circle in that particular chapter of my life. Of course, I still enjoy the academic environment and remain involved at the Architectural Association, where I hold the head of design position. My best tip for learners of all kinds is to continuously embrace a student's mindset. Be confident in your abilities, but don't assume that you know anything.

NATIVE INSTRUMENTS

KOMPLETE Audio 2
TRAKTOR S3
MASCHINE Mikro

How do you find solutions that address a brand's true needs? Our branding process begins with an immersion phase, where we conduct a comprehensive brand audit and formulate a branding strategy. We present our findings and work to come to a mutual understanding with our clients before beginning the design stage. Our ideas then go through various verification steps to ensure they are consistent with the overall direction.

For example, we recently finalized a project with Native Instruments, a company known for developing and distributing music software products aimed at sound engineers, musicians, and DJs. Many of its individual products had gained more recognition than the parent brand itself. In order to conceive a cohesive branding experience, it was crucial to ensure that its products, like Maschine, Traktor, and Komplete, were as recognizable as the main brand. And so we developed a distinctive variable typeface that incorporated distinct visual expressions for certain glyphs, such as N, M, K, and R. Our comprehensive solution included a new symbol, a logo system for all of their products, and an overarching visual language.

In the past, you have mentioned the importance of being both a creator and a translator. How do you achieve that balance? Finding the right balance is key in every design project, but there is no one-size-fits-all formula. It's a delicate dance between meeting the project requirements and injecting innovation and a personal touch that leads to success. That elusive sweet spot is what sets exceptional design work apart.

3 — POSTER DESIGN FOR A BAUHAUS-ARCHIV DESIGN
TALK AT THE CENTRE POMPIDOU
4 — LOGOTYPE AND TYPEFACE DESIGN
FOR NATIVE INSTRUMENTS

TYPOGRAPHY—A bespoke typeface, the bedrock of Lobe's work for Adam Katz Sinding, provides a balanced combination of contrast, stroke, and depth for the American-born, Copenhagen-based photographer's three names. A blend of American Gothic and 20th-century European Neo-Grotesk typefaces reflect the fashion zeitgeist of the decade, thus providing a bold and confident foundation for the visual identity to be positioned at eye level with other brands.

Paris Fashion Week
Haute Couture FW'23 THOM BROWNE
ADAM KATZ SINDING

FRA LHR
JFK SYD
MAD HKG
BER BCN
ALX ZHR
COP AKS

5

6   7

5 — KEY VISUALS FOR ADAM KATZ SINDING
6 — TYPOGRAPHY FOR ADAM KATZ SINDING
7 — ADAM KATZ SINDING LAUNCH CAMPAIGN

Each project comes with its own set of challenges and objectives. A thoughtful approach is imperative to understanding the problem at hand and devising creative solutions. It's about going beyond the surface level and delving deeper into the essence of the project, uncovering insights, and exploring new possibilities. Innovation plays a vital role. It brings a sense of novelty and captivates the audience, leaving a lasting impact. As designers, we should embrace technological advancements and view them as opportunities. At the same time, infusing a personal touch is crucial. Adding that special ingredient makes the design memorable, and reflective of the client's vision and values. It's about knowing that target audience and crafting an experience that connects with them on a deeper level.

Our primary focus is on capturing personality, fostering uniqueness, and evoking emotional responses. Whether a project strikes a chord on a local or global scale becomes inconsequential when it possesses these key attributes. Virgil Abloh once said that he always worked with his 17-year-old self in mind, and that sentiment resonates deeply with me. If that young kid in me doesn't get excited, something is missing.

A direct nod to the architecture of the Bibliothèque Nationale du Luxembourg (BNL), Lobe devised a flexible block system, which allows the library staff to easily make changes to its signage.

8 9

10

8 — MODULAR WAYFINDING SYSTEM FOR BNL
9 — DETAILS OF FLOOR NUMBERS FOR BNL
10 — RESIN CUBES FOR BNL'S SIGNAGE

STUDIO
ATELIER DYAKOVA

CLIENT
PAPER FOUNDATION

YEAR
2020

Atelier Dyakova
Paper Foundation

CREATIVE DIRECTION
SONYA DYAKOVA

GRAPHIC DESIGN
TOM BABER
GABRIELLA VOYIAS

PHOTOGRAPHY
LOUIS ROGERS
ED PARK

Sometimes the best way to move forward is to look back, so when Atelier Dyakova's team was tasked with developing an identity for Paper Foundation, a charitable organization and papermaker based in northern England's Lake District, they dug deep into its roots.

"Time and time again, I see meaningful results from genuine research, in-person site visits, and face-to-face conversations," says Sonya Dyakova. In order to develop an intimate connection with her client, she boarded a train with her team from London to the picturesque village of Burneside, Cumbria, where their client is based. Created by Mark Cropper, a sixth-generation papermaker and chair of the renowned James Cropper mill, Paper Foundation's premises immediately inspired its visitors, who were awestruck by Cropper's

dedication to sharing knowledge, reviving skills, preserving physical tools and processes, and involving the local community.

Having been immersed in the paper mill's history, as well as its part in printing some of the first telegrams ever sent, Dyakova says she also reveled in its "rich archive of printed ephemera." In turn, this led Atelier Dyakova to research the typography of the industrial revolution, searching for the right visual answer. An envelope featuring an all-caps sans-serif typeface with a distinctive underline and period was exactly what they were looking for. "Returning from the Lake District only days before the pandemic lockdowns, I knew this humble object held the key to our solution," remembers Dyakova. Printed by James Cropper in

the 1800s, the telegram envelope, with its eccentric layout and details, became the basis for Paper Foundation's wordmark. The studio adopted the letter's distinguishing typographic treatment and crafted bespoke letterforms, employing similar weighting, proportions, and spacing. The agency also created Burneside Grotesque, a custom typeface loosely based on Grotesque No. 6 by the 19th-century Stephenson Blake company in Sheffield, to accompany it. "We aimed to provide a simple and meaningful solution that would bridge the organization's activities steeped in heritage and their resolute look towards the future," says Dyakova. With a desire to explore and the will to leave no stone unturned, she and her team accomplished their goal.

PAPER FOUNDATION.

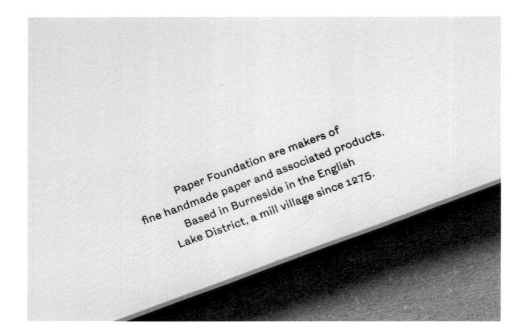

Paper Foundation are makers of fine handmade paper and associated products. Based in Burneside in the English Lake District, a mill village since 1275.

INSPIRATION FOR THE
PAPER FOUNDATION WORDMARK

PAPER FOUNDATION.

PHYSICAL —Printed by the Baddeley Brothers on stock from the Japanese paper specialist Takeo, Paper Foundation's business cards echo the tactility of handmade paper. Atelier Dyakova wanted these cards to evoke the process of working with, and compressing, recycled material or pulp into the tray.

The stylized emblem of a home is a symbol of the organization's aspiration of being a protected and safe space where skills are nurtured and an archive can flourish.

A B C D F G H I
J K L M N O P Q R
S T U V W X Y Z
0 1 2 3 4 5 6 7 8 9

Ss

Pigmented Jumbo Roll Kraft Pulp

As to paper, it seems to be generally adm
that the kind called, and to some extent
called, 'hand made' is the best if only bec
most durable. Of this there are, accordir
sort of mould used in the making, two kir
'laid', (made in a mould formed of fine me
running longitudinally, with stronger trar
wires at considerably greater intervals), ;
'wove' (made in a mould of woven metal f
this distinction there are two things to be
first, that hand made wove paper can onl

BURNESIDE GROTESQUE, A BESPOKE
TYPEFACE FOR PAPER FOUNDATION

Paper Foundation, Ellergreen, Burneside, Kendal, LA9 5SD, England

STUDIO   CLIENT   YEAR
1/1 STUDIO   JESS HANNAH   2017

1/1 Studio
J. Hannah

CREATIVE DIRECTION   EDITORIAL STRATEGY   PHOTOGRAPHY
NATASHA SAWICKI MEAD   LEIGH PATTERSON   STELLA BERKOFSKY
                                                                          JESSI FREDERICK

GRAPHIC DESIGN   NATALIE THOMPSON
NATASHA SAWICKI MEAD   JOSHUA BRIONES-YAP

From her very first conversations with Jess Hannah, founder of the jewelry company J. Hannah, and Leigh Patterson, the creative director charged with its editorial strategy, Natasha Sawicki Mead knew that it would be vital to create a common language. "We shared all of the things our minds cannot help but wander back to," the Auckland-based designer recalls. "The J. Hannah collections contextualize the timelessly familiar with the contemporary, pairing jewelry with references from art history, color theory, and modern culture."

By compiling their collective creative inspirations, 1/1 Studio laid the foundation to pursue a design guided by a mix of interdisciplinary references: the jewelry's rich heritage, time-steeped symbolism, and esoteric color references. Mead and her team developed an identity that could house this archival material, creating a

visual language supporting both long- and short-form storytelling across print and digital applications. "These brand stories reflect a culture that is not just seen but felt in the imagination," says Mead.

Her job, then, was to bring that imaginative spirit to life in a tangible way. She did so by establishing a wordmark with an engraved and hand-finished quality to reflect the craft behind the jewelry itself.

Drawing from classic makers' marks, and using the palindrome from the brand name to create a symmetrical design, Mead's team also developed a monogram as a secondary logo. "We then chose Folio for its historical familiarity and warmth," the designer says of J. Hannah's primary typeface. "It evokes nostalgia without pinning itself to a particular period, telling a more universal story of understatement and grace." The type becomes

recognizable in the overall identity, but doesn't overpower any other element.

When the collection grew to include a line of carefully edited, high-quality nail polishes, J. Hannah entrusted 1/1 Studio to seamlessly integrate the new products into the existing offering. Mead notes that the design language, "inspired by artists' palettes and natural elements," was extended to include visual color libraries or charts for each shade. She devised a polish bottle based on a nostalgic 1990s rectangle form in a weighty glass, further emphasizing J. Hannah's trademark aesthetic: classic yet distinctive, refined yet playful. "The key to ensuring that the brand, jewelry, and polish are in harmony and that the design aligns with the overall business," Mead concludes, "is a partnership built on mutual creative respect and inspiration."

THE SYMMETRICAL LOGO,
A PLAY ON THE PALINDROME

PHYSICAL —The jewelry packaging, developed in collaboration with Heavy Atelier, is designed to be a keepsake for each piece. The rigid box, which is finished with a white-foiled monogram on top, includes a letterpressed insert and a reusable cloth dust bag for travel.

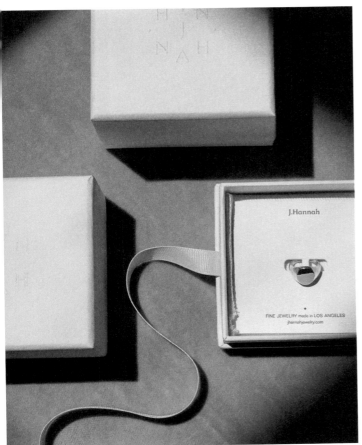

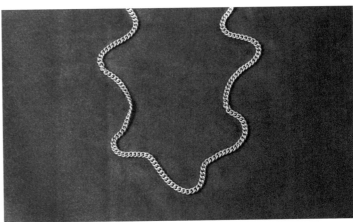

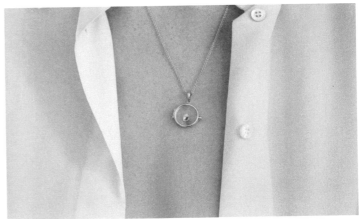

DIGITAL — Quick to recognize the storytelling potential of platforms like Instagram, Jess Hannah and Leigh Patterson crafted an online presence fostering deeper community connections as their brand's online cornerstone.

"Through this, we sought digital applications designed with editorial substance and grace, all while retaining notes of irreverence and personality," says Mead.

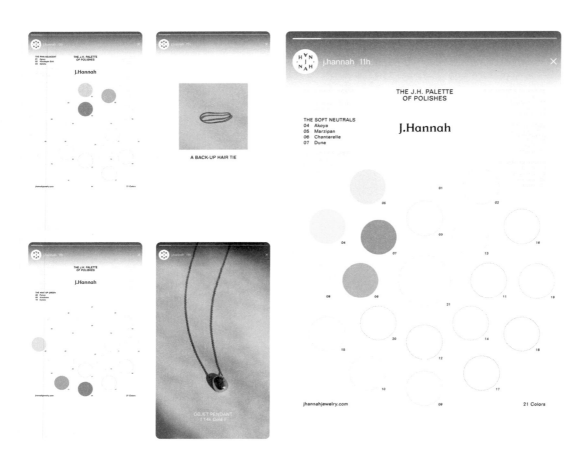

THE SOFT HUES THAT DEFINE J. HANNAH
EXTEND ACROSS ITS DIGITAL CHANNELS

J.Hannah

SHOP
Jewelry
Rings
Earrings
Necklaces
Bracelets

In-Stock
Personalized
Limited Editions
Sale
Modern Antiquities
Signet
Dress
Lacé
Identity
Charm
Classics

Nailpolish
Etcetera

INFO
JOURNAL
LOOKBOOK
SEARCH

Carob

PRICE: $22

DETAILS –

Rich coffee. Bittersweet. Black walnut.

A line of carefully-edited, high quality polishes for the color-resistant. Polishes that consider the gracefulness of hands, and the role of subtle color as an element in the considered wardrobe. All polishes are non-toxic, cruelty-free and made in the USA.

Nail polish is final sale.

FREE FROM +
INGREDIENTS +
SHIPPING & RETURNS +

Ask a question

ADD TO CART | $22

Influences

Carob

1.   Pain Aux Chocolat

2.   Claude Lalanne's brooch, 1996

Carob
Influences

Inspired by artists' palettes, natural elements, and the muses who we envision channeling specific colors or moods.

Rich coffee.
Bittersweet.
Black walnut.

SHOP
ALL POLISH

Newsletter Sign Up

Subscribe

Shipping
Returns
Refund policy

Instagram
Pinterest
Facebook

Contact
Terms of service
Privacy Policy

© J. Hannah
Made in Los Angeles
Site by 1/1

DIRECTION—Like J. Hannah's Glacé collection, which could seemingly belong to any era yet manages to make a modern statement, Mead's lookbook design exudes timelessness while fitting squarely into the present by weaving images of the jewelry with historical references.

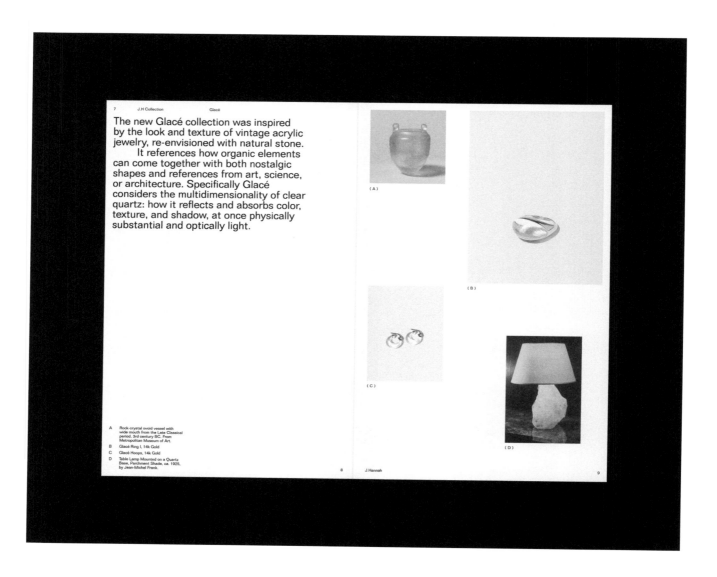

7   J.H Collection   Glacé

The new Glacé collection was inspired by the look and texture of vintage acrylic jewelry, re-envisioned with natural stone.
    It references how organic elements can come together with both nostalgic shapes and references from art, science, or architecture. Specifically Glacé considers the multidimensionality of clear quartz: how it reflects and absorbs color, texture, and shadow, at once physically substantial and optically light.

(A)

(B)

(C)

(D)

A   Rock-crystal ovoid vessel with wide mouth from the Late Classical period, 3rd century BC. From Metropolitan Museum of Art.
B   Glacé Ring I, 14k Gold
C   Glacé Hoops, 14k Gold
D   Table Lamp Mounted on a Quartz Base, Parchment Shade, ca. 1925, by Jean-Michel Frank.

8   J.Hannah   9

THE DEBOSSED LOGO ON OFF-WHITE TEXTURED
PAPER REINFORCES THE BRAND'S AESTHETIC

HANNAH
J.
HANNAH

II

Direction

On Making the Map

Ideation
& Conception

In Debbie Millman's book *How to Think Like a Great Graphic Designer,* the writer, curator, educator, and host of the *Design Matters* podcast likens effective design to "wizardry of sorts," breaking through what she refers to as "the modern-day chaos of sensory overload." Millman penned these words in 2007, the same year that Apple released the iPhone and before the internet truly existed in our pockets, whereupon an always-connected way of life became the norm for nearly everyone across the globe. All this to say, if Millman thought that design was wizardry then, it certainly is now. So how do we go on to construct an identity that is persuasive, meaningful, and stands the test of time? Solid and thoughtful direction, for one.

"Art direction," writes Millman, "is the translator between a brand's strategy and its visual expression." In an open, competitive marketplace, where products and services are increasingly democratized and almost everything is commodified, the way in which a brand's offerings are communicated visually, and shaped experientially, can be the determining factor for success. Coming from discovery, we designers and strategists have to once again resist our urges to jump directly into the design phase and instead give this translation period the time it deserves.

As with almost any creative endeavor, there are no hard-and-fast rules here. Techniques differ between individuals, studios, and, of course, projects. Take Mirko Borsche, the award-winning German designer and creative director. In a 2021 episode of the *Creative Voyage* podcast, he discusses his own approach. Suggesting that he isn't afraid of client input ("The more both sides are open to discussion—the better the output."), he nevertheless notes that the concept of art direction has radically changed during his career—and will continue to evolve too. "All of my tasks, the things we do, have shifted," he explains. "But in the end, it's all about guiding a product or creative leads in the right direction for a brand."

Such directorial processes often begin with additional research and development. With the creative brief as our compass, we build upon the approved goals, initial design requirements, and overall strategy to identify the visual and verbal language that the brand will ultimately adopt. We look deeper into the specific project or the niche that the brand is working within. We start to explore creative concepts and begin sketching, creating mood boards, or conceiving initial logo ideas. We might even look into typographic possibilities, color palettes, or imagery styles. "We want the client to be able to change something without totally killing the idea," Borsche says aptly. Whether we have involved the client or not, we keep it loose, and we keep it open. We brainstorm within the studio, but we also seek outside input, consulting a colleague or a trusted specialist.

Direction can stop at internal decks that inform our work on design proposals, or it can be deeply intertwined in the creation of these first proposals themselves. We might begin crafting initial visual identity options—it's typical to present three—that showcase different, yet relevant solutions. Focusing on elements like graphic design, illustration, and typography, we can create early mockups so that the client can envision their brand in the world and entertain different possibilities. This moment is one of many where we can address the client's own creative inclinations and insecurities. The sooner that we understand where they want to go and how, the better we will be able to guide them to their destination. It's how we enhance trust and foster a spirit of collaboration.

However we choose to approach this stage, the results should be rooted in three ways: dedication to the project goal, a concept and context-based creative vision, and a bird's-eye view of all the moving parts in the execution process. The word "direction" implies progress, momentum, a path towards something else, and our job is to make that something else great. Without this phase, we may very well just sit still.

Hector Muelas

Diving inside the Mind of a Distinguished Creative Director

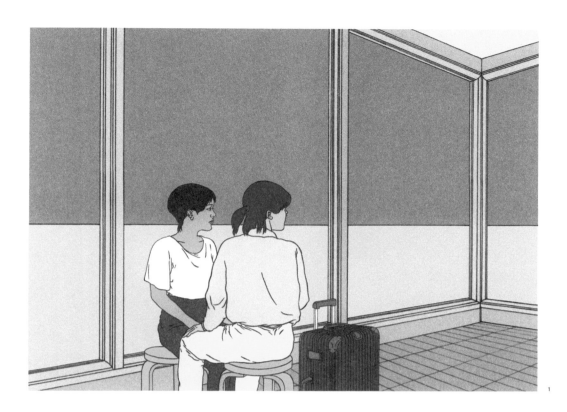

In 2018, Muelas conceived the "Travel with Purpose" campaign for Rimowa. The collaboration with London-based illustrator Manshen Lo and Parisian art director Yannis Henrion resulted in three artworks, one of which was later displayed in the luggage manufacturer's flagship Hong Kong store.

Hector Muelas has an impressive resume: Apple's creative director, LVMH's content and creative vice president, Rimowa's chief brand officer, the Expedia Group's senior marketing and creative vice president, and now the chief brand creative officer at Tiffany & Co. Which is to say, this man knows a thing or two about brands. Yet when asked about his origin story, he laughs. "I'm not sure how I got here," he replies. His path, he explains, was far from linear, veering from journalism to advertising to entertainment, luxury, and technology.

He considers attributing his wayward journey to his childhood. Raised in Barcelona, he watched his father transition from lawyer to windsurf shop owner. "I grew up at the intersection of those two narratives," he says, "the rigor of law—with its systems and arguments—and the creativity of community-driven cultures."

Muelas still isn't certain that these experiences set him apart, but he agrees that they made way for him to become "neither pure creative, nor pure marketer." Consciously in the middle, he instead serves business objectives and solves problems by taking time to really understand them and then devising innovative solutions in response.

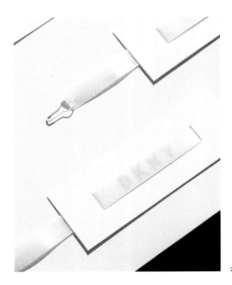

2

He draws inspiration from those who he calls "the OG brand builders," such as Dan Wieden and David Kennedy, Steve Jobs, and Lee Clow. Their methodology, in his eyes, is bulletproof, and not too dissimilar from that of a journalist or lawyer. "Find a brand's purpose," Muelas elaborates. "Don't ever manufacture it. Dig and dig until you find the truth—a human truth. And then build an emotionally compelling argument around it."

For Muelas, this approach means strategy at every turn. He begins by asking questions: What is this brand's purpose? How does it deliver that purpose? What are its codes, or its vehicles? He finds answers by way of intense research. "I like to nerd out with history and explore category tropes," he muses. When working on the rebrand of luxury German luggage company Rimowa with its chief executive Alexandre Arnault and the team at London-based branding consultancy Commission Studio, he dove headfirst into the luggage company's storied past. In doing so, he uncovered forgotten events like a fire that engulfed its factory and the iconic ridges of the Cologne Cathedral that sits opposite its flagship store, as well as the brand's legacy of rich graphic language.

To determine the overall direction, Muelas and his team put a brand book and manifesto together to clearly define Rimowa's mission and values. "These assets made the decisions clearer," he insists. "We had a guiding principle instead of the dreaded, 'I like this, I don't like that.' Everyone involved knew how to evaluate what was the right thing for Rimowa, rather than letting their personal taste get in the way." The final outcome, a masterful blend of the contemporary with the traditional, of the luxurious and the utilitarian, included an all-new monogram, typography suite, packaging system, and even a collaboration with Virgil Abloh's Off-White.

Along with an internal team, external partners like Commission Studio and fellow London favorite Any Other Name allow Muelas to bring his visions to life. "I always look for strong strategic and conceptual skills, obsession around craft, and good cultural taste," he says. He likens Commission Studio to an extension of his own brain, one that simultaneously offers different perspectives and points of view.

While any given project can take many forms, Muelas scoffs at the idea of remaining current. "There are millions of parallel cultural universes happening at the same time," he says. Instead, he aims to create identities that are built with longevity, consistency, and thoughtfulness in mind from day one. "They can scale, evolve, or devolve, but they always stay true to their foundations." Storytelling, for example, is imperative for strong brand architecture, but he shies away from anything overly grandiose.

2 — PRODUCT COLLATERAL FOR DKNY
3 — REFRESHED PACKAGING SYSTEM
    FOR THE HARMONIST

3

In partnership with Commission Studio, Muelas devised a brand refresh including a revised packaging suite for the Paris-based fragrance house The Harmonist. Each scent is accompanied by a unique illustration inspired by the Aesthetic Movement, which flourished in England in the late 1800s.

Thinking back to his days at Apple, Muelas recalls working on the identity for its streaming service Apple Music, a platform launched thanks in part to the record executive and entrepreneur Jimmy Iovine. "He shows up one day and tells us that he wants Apple Music to be the place where music lives," Muelas remembers, "just like in the 1980s when people believed that musicians actually lived in MTV." Muelas took Iovine's words to heart and developed a flexible framework that allowed artists to bring their own stories to the table, rather than pushing dominant brand assets dictated clearly by the in-house team. Muelas describes the result as "a blank canvas for storytelling where the actual Apple Music wordmark became an element within the worlds created by these incredible artists."

With a hand in so many iconic operations, there's no doubt that Muelas plays an important role. But what does it mean to be a brand officer or a creative director? Simply put, he says, the answer is "a human being responsible for defining the systems, processes, and behaviors that make a brand." Of course, the reality is a little more complicated than that. His job is to study and understand the essence of a brand and then build an ever-evolving operative system from it so that the brand can scale across channels and platforms. "It is someone who threads that system into the fabric of culture," he continues. "And finally, someone that knows how and when to release that operative system into the wild, so that communities can also be a part of it." Perhaps most importantly, his profession requires him to shield brands from creating what he calls "visual pollution." If one thing is certain, it's that whatever Muelas chooses to let loose into the landscape—the complex ecosystem of both physical and digital content—will be deliberate and deeply considered.

4

5

Muelas employed Commission Studio to craft an updated Rimowa identity that better reflects the company's highly considered customer experience. Having developed a reimagined wordmark with Bureau Borsche, they then sought the help of Imprimerie du Marais to ensure that the tiniest of details were preserved across its physical collateral, including stickers, hang tags, and manuals.

4 — LUGGAGE TAGS FOR RIMOWA
5 — PRINT COLLATERAL FOR RIMOWA
6 — UPDATED OWNER'S MANUAL FOR RIMOWA

MOUTHWASH Studio

Before becoming real-life collaborators, Abraham Campillo, Alex Tan, and Mackenzie Freemire were merely friends online. They dreamed up Mouthwash as an off-hours podcast and print publication—a means to simultaneously stay in touch with each other and to connect with like-minded makers and movers. Progressing rapidly from a side hustle to a fully-fledged enterprise, the trio handed in resignations to their respective agencies in 2019 and never looked back. With a team of 14, an office in Los Angeles, and a new research center that provides a dedicated space for unfettered exploration, Campillo, Tan, Freemire, and their newest partner Ben Mingo have learned to expect the unexpected— or simply put, that moving in the same direction isn't always the best policy.

1

2

3

When conceiving a brand identity, how do you settle on a general direction? What does your creative process look like? It involves an incredible amount of research, not only digesting and referencing the context and history in the area of interest, but forecasting and looking at adjacent industries to understand how they tackle similar problems. While direction may be broadly viewed as just that first half, digesting and referencing, we really see the magic in the latter half where we discern what the most essential elements are among all of the competing distractions. Everything gets more interesting when you have contrasting ideas living side by side. Brands are never just one thing or one thought, so we always look to unlock the identity through these combinations. What if this architecture studio looked like a fashion house? What if this technology company sounded like a children's brand?

Our research almost always comes in the form of mixed media. We reference print publications, YouTube videos, academic reports, random Wikipedia articles, and anything we can get our hands on in an attempt to become as expert as we can in whatever field we are working in. We compile that research alongside our discovery, and our team starts discussing what directions we are interested in exploring. It's a conversation not just reserved for designers. Our whole team—art directors, strategists, producers, copywriters—is involved. While there's always a risk of having too many cooks in the kitchen, we have found a way to keep the process collaborative, transparent, and inviting for the entire team as well as the client. Everyone comes to the table with new and diverse ideas. It's what makes each project feel different, each solution feel unique.

What questions often go neglected in the branding process? You can have the most beautiful logomark, the sleekest custom typeface, the most reactive motion design system, and none of it matters if the container it lives in isn't made for it. It's really the context surrounding the identity that can be overlooked or undervalued. Most of us tend to fixate on the visuals in front of us, but there's so much going on behind the scenes that impacts the perception of a brand. Does the product feel good in my hands? Does the digital experience improve my day-to-day life or make things easier for me somehow? Is the content inspiring? Does it stop me in my tracks? Does the copy illuminate me and provide some sort of understanding that I didn't have before? If the visual identity looks amazing but you're missing the mark on all of those other aspects, it becomes increasingly hard to justify the brand.

1 — A REFRESHED IDENTITY FOR THE UTAH JAZZ
2 — KINETIC TYPE FOR THE UTAH JAZZ REBRAND
3 — UPDATED UTAH JAZZ UNIFORM

DIGITAL—With a roster that includes some of today's most forward-thinking visual artists, Artworld required an identity where these creatives take center stage and its own brand elements hold strong in the background.

A reimagined website puts equal emphasis on individual work as it does the entire collection, encouraging Artworld's clients to intuitively find artists for specific projects.

4 — A SELECTION OF WORK ON THE ARTWORLD WEBSITE
5 — UPDATED TYPOGRAPHIC IDENTITY FOR ARTWORLD
6 — DIGITAL ARTIST PORTFOLIOS FOR ARTWORLD

tographer: Marc Hibbert
ing: Ib Kamara
ting: Mischa Notcutt
e-up: Thom Walker

c.hibbert@gmail.com
chibbert.com

Maximilian AW21   08/14

21 June 2021   Publication: Revue Magazine
                    Photographer: Chieska Fortuna Smith
                    Location: New York, NY 2021

                    hello@roxanedia.de
                    roxanedia.de

Roxane Dia   Revue Beauté

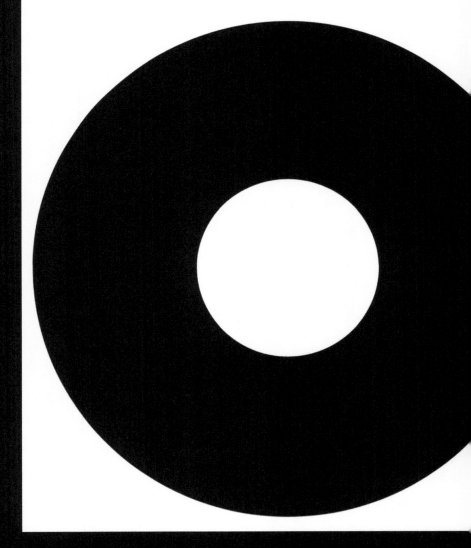

Generally speaking, how has branding shifted? How does that impact your studio work? With the spaces we're operating in changing as rapidly as they do, we're seeing the need for brands and experiences to transform. Almost nothing is static anymore. And anything that is finds itself at a severe disadvantage.

The balance lies in creating dynamic experiences that don't feel superfluous. The goal is always to elevate rather than decorate. Take the Neutra VDL project. We could have come in and made a beautiful brand identity that was rich with references from the midcentury modern movement and completely missed the bigger picture of what we actually wanted to achieve—opening this experience to more people than the original movement ever made possible.

We don't just settle for solutions that may have previously worked, and we constantly try new things, continuing to challenge how we present ideas to clients, how case studies are shared through social, or where the work lives and is circulated. Motion development has been a profound element in our creative process, bringing our ideas from 2D into 3D to develop reactive identity systems. To us, it's as much a vehicle for storytelling as a logomark or brand narrative.

How do you ensure that a brand's identity is flexible enough to adapt to changing trends and market conditions? That's the golden question, isn't it? We try to get closer to a point of future-proofing by asking, "Where do you imagine yourself in one year? Three years? Five?" or "What do you want to introduce that you haven't been able to figure out yet?"

It isn't enough to just talk about these things. We actually have to deliver on these conversations. As much as we might not like it, concepts end up changing once we start defining how they will look and feel. We're constantly revisiting our strategy and direction to make sure it's landing where it needs to. It's quite an iterative, nonlinear process requiring an empathetic perspective most of the time. Who *needs* to be experiencing this? Is this what they need to hear and see? Is this the best place for them to be receiving it? Maintaining that empathetic approach is the best way to ensure that the work will grow with its audience.

In your eyes, what defines a truly excellent visual identity? If there were objective truths to what we were doing, then there would only be exceptional work out there—and obviously, that isn't the case. For us, the goal has always been to make work that ages well and positively impacts people. While it's impossible to guarantee those results, we sincerely approach things one day at a time and hope for the best.

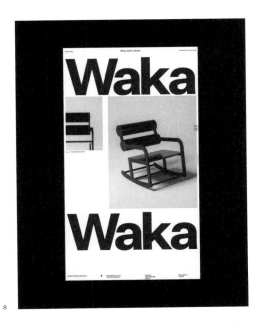

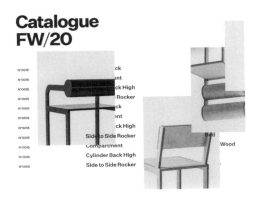

7
8
9

7 — FULL-SCREEN IMAGERY FEATURING
    WAKA WAKA CHAIR
8 — NEW DIGITAL IDENTITY FOR WAKA WAKA
9 — WAKA WAKA ONLINE CATALOG

DEVEAUX
NEW YORK

Through details in typography, interactive design in product pages, and a built-in digital moodboard, Mouthwash devised a system that allows Deveaux to express itself while remaining true to its minimalist visual core.

We believe that all great things have a degree of simplicity that allows them to cut through the noise. There should be a level of play involved, too. In a world of transaction and optimization, a bit of playful interaction goes a really long way. And tending to move in the opposite direction of everyone else does work sometimes.

But it's best not to take these things too seriously. The moment you set out to make something seriously excellent is when it all starts to fall apart. So we just make the work that we want to see, and we sing and dance a little in between.

10 11

12

10 — DEVEAUX NEW YORK CAMPAIGN WITH CUSTOM TYPEFACE
11 — BRAND PHOTOGRAPHY FOR DEVEAUX NEW YORK
12 — DEVEAUX NEW YORK'S E-COMMERCE PLATFORM

STUDIO   CLIENT   YEAR
BIELKE&YANG   NORDIC HOTELS   2022
                  & RESORTS

Bielke&Yang
Sommerro

ART DIRECTION   MARTIN YANG
EVAN MCGUINNESS   CHRISTIAN BIELKE

GRAPHIC DESIGN   MOTION DESIGN   PHOTOGRAPHY
MORTEN HÅVIK   STEVEN REDWOOD   LARS PETTER PETTERSEN

ADVISING   TYPE DESIGN   ILLUSTRATION
AKSEL OVERSKOTT   BOBBY TANNAM   BENDIK KALTENBORN

When Christian Bielke and Martin Yang set out to develop the identity for Oslo's Sommerro Hotel, they knew that they were taking on more than just another hospitality project. "We needed to communicate a familiar concept—the hotel—in a new way," they explain.

The parent group, Nordic Hotels and Resorts, envisioned the building as a neighborhood meeting ground in the Norwegian capital. Honing the brand's strategy, narrative, and visual character over the course of nearly four years before the grand opening, Bielke and Yang tried to emphasize the idea that the hotel functions as a "community house open to everyone." Set in the restored former headquarters of the city's electrical company, Oslo Lysverker, the project's heart lies in the juxtaposition of old and new, classic and modern, with an emphasis on community. When it came to the brand's primary colors of dark red, ochre, and beige, as well as its overall aesthetics, the Bielke&Yang team looked to the landmark building, designed by Georg Eliassen and Andreas Bjercke in 1917 and built in 1931, for inspiration.

An ode to the structure's original working name, To Søstre (Two Sisters), and the women featured in the Per Krogh mosaic housed inside, the logo epitomizes the brand's mission of reopening a historic site to the public while placing visitors at its center. "The typeface is the result of a comprehensive study of the Art Deco movement," reveal Bielke and Yang. "Since Sommerro itself was to become a meeting point for people from both the surrounding neighborhood of Frogner and the rest of the world, we wanted to capture this international movement in one family." The bespoke typeface, designed with Bobby Tannam, features a diverse array of ligatures and glyphs, and as such can be adjusted in seemingly unlimited ways. This critical element means that sub-brands, like bars, restaurants, and the bathhouse, can diversify while remaining recognizable. Having a hand in everything from signage to amenities, wayfinding, and digital assets, Bielke&Yang signatures are omnipresent in Sommerro's new identity, making it the studio's most rewarding—yet challenging project—to date. Indeed, they haven't just refreshed the hotel's branding. As the studio's founders suggest, they have created "an entirely new genre in Norway's hospitality sector."

SOMMERRO

THE ART DECO AESTHETIC IS
CENTRAL TO SOMMERRO'S IDENTITY

"Illustrations add a sense of play, allowing the identity to be toned up or down, making both families and businesspeople feel at home," say Bielke and Yang.

To create everything from whimsical wool seat covers to embroidered curtains and a series of postcards for Sommerro, they partnered with Norwegian artist Bendik Kaltenborn.

DETAIL OF SEAT COVER DREAMED UP BY
BIELKE&YANG AND BENDIK KALTENBORN

PHYSICAL — Sometimes printed matter is the best way to share a story, so Bielke&Yang collaborated with photographers, writers, and Sommerro's key contributors to produce *A New Era,* a 360-page tome. The book, which can be purchased at the hotel, is a tangible way for visitors to connect with the project and its carefully crafted brand narrative.

EACH OF THE VARIANTS WITHIN THE CUSTOM
TYPE FAMILY OFFERS ITS OWN TWIST

SOMMERRO
A NEW ERA

STUDIO
TRIC

CLIENT
HERRON FAMILY

YEAR
2019

TRiC
Hillwood

CREATIVE DIRECTION
TRISTAN CEDDIA
RICK MILOVANOVIC

COPYWRITING
HAYLEY MCKEE

PRINT PRODUCTION
TAYLOR'D PRESS

PACKAGING PHOTOGRAPHY
DANIEL HERRMANN-ZOLL

LIFESTYLE PHOTOGRAPHY
JOSH ROBENSTONE

TYPOGRAPHY
SELF MODERN BY BRETAGNE

Every brand has a story to tell, but they don't all begin on the banks of the Tamar River in northern Tasmania, Australia. Here, Paul Herron of the Tamar Valley Distillery with help from his triplet sons, Daniel, Joel, and Oliver, crafts small-batch, single malt whisky from what they believe is the purest water on Earth. Their product, hinged on an obsession with quality at every turn, emerged into the world as an instant classic under the creative direction of TRiC, run by Tristan Ceddia, Rick Milovanovic, and their studio team.

When seeking visual guidance for their signature Hillwood Whisky, a tipple named after their beloved rural town where there are "no shops and no interruptions," the Herrons connected with TRiC via a childhood friend of the sons. Sometimes things just click, and TRiC quickly set about presenting the Herron family's labor of love to the world.

Through a series of deep discussions as well as an in-person visit, TRiC came to appreciate just how rooted Hillwood is in its local community. "Hillwood stands out as a premium product," notes Ceddia, "that embodies the essence of its unique location." In an effort to emulate the brand's timelessness, TRiC shifted focus away from the wide world of whisky, which can lean heavily on heritage and vintage tropes, and looked for inspiration in fragrance packaging instead. Their carefully fashioned bespoke wordmark, derived from a tweaked Adobe system font, further asserts Hillwood's refined feel. Complementing the elegant typographic elements, the "HH" logo portrays the interlocked initials of Hillwood and Herron. While maintaining the same visual simplicity, it playfully employs an Easter egg story element.

"The monogram features three vertical strokes symbolizing the triplet sons connected by one horizontal stroke, representing their father," explains Ceddia. The embossed wordmark married with the logo's softer watermark is carefully translated onto off-white textured paper, leaving room for each bottle's specifics to be hand-finished by Paul Herron.

"By eschewing gimmicks and fancy finishes, the labels remain clean and unadorned, much like the whisky itself," Ceddia declares. Like the pristine water that is filtered through 250-million-year-old rock formations before it is used to create Hillwood, the most powerful things are often the simplest. From the physical manifestation of the product to the distillery's digital channels, TRiC's work reflects the family's core values: slowing down and getting back to the basics.

Tasmanian Single Malt Whisky
Tamar Valley Distillery

HILLWOOD

Single Cask Matured
Alc.Vol. 61.4% 500mL

HILLWOOD

THE ELEGANT, YET STORY-RICH WORD-
MARK AND MONOGRAM FOR HILLWOOD

PHYSICAL— For bottling, the Herron family sourced simple, weighty receptacles with clean lines. Finished with a wooden stopper, the grain variation provides another unique touch to each bottle, which is then housed in a handmade beech wood box artfully created by Brendon Herron, Paul Herron's brother.

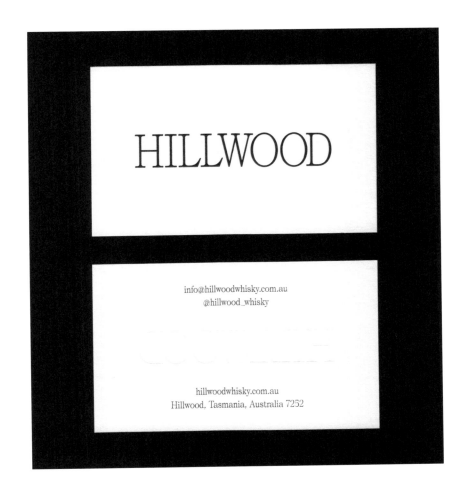

A SIMPLE BUSINESS CARD IS ACCENTUATED
BY THE DEBOSSED WORDMARK

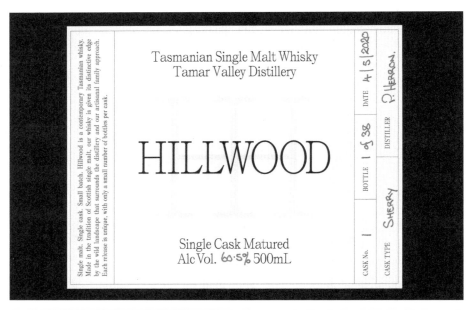

Gently filtered through glacial rock deposited over 250 million years ago.

HILLWOOD EMPHASIZES PURITY FROM ITS
VISUAL ASSETS TO THE PRODUCT ITSELF

HILLWOOD

III

Typography

Language in Form

Lettering & Type Design

As far back as the pictorial signs inscribed on clay tablets in Mesopotamia, writing has been, alongside speech and image-making and music, one of the most essential forms for human communication, and fundamentally, branding *is* communication. We must therefore constantly consider how a brand conveys the written word, and typography—the art of arranging type to make written language legible, readable, and appealing when displayed—is our medium.

"Typography is not only a technology but is itself a natural resource or staple, like cotton or timber or radio," writes media theorist Marshall McLuhan in his 1962 book *The Gutenberg Galaxy.* Since Johannes Gutenberg, the printing press innovator often attributed as the very first typographer himself, typefaces have become to designers what clay is to sculptors and bricks to builders. In essence, they allow us to convey a brand's tone, personality, and values in subtle yet incredibly effective ways.

A well-rounded typographic system should be versatile and functional, while still having a unique and memorable style that can distinguish the brand in its given niche. Type may not always play an obvious leading role like a brand's photography or color palette. In fact, its job is sometimes best done when it becomes nearly invisible, quietly swaying our visual strategies. Typography, for example, might not be the first thing that enters the consciousness of an average MacBook user. Yet, it was high on the mind of Apple founder Steve Jobs, who studied calligraphy in the 1970s and learned about serif and sans-serif typefaces, letter spacing, and the general principles behind great type systems. "And we designed it all into the Mac," he went on to say. "It was the first computer with beautiful typography." We—much like Jobs and Susan Kare, the graphic designer responsible for these early Macintosh iterations—cannot overlook type's power to educate and engage.

We begin by making selections. We consider a brand's target audience, their overall aesthetic, and last but not least, functionality. We ask, "What impression does a brand want to portray?" We look to serif typefaces, which can express a sense of tradition and elegance, or sans-serif options that suggest modernity and simplicity, for our answers. We might opt for a variable typeface, a single font file that contains multiple alternatives for characteristics like weight, width, and slant. Or perhaps we consider developing a bespoke typeface altogether, which can give a brand its unique edge or lend to a more cohesive and distinctive visual identity. We might also implement a logotype that is purely typographic. For instance, when employing initialisms or abbreviations rather than a full name, such solutions are often referred to as "wordmarks" or "monograms." This process, however, doesn't stop with these choices. We also need to create a dynamic typographic hierarchy that can satisfy all imaginable use cases, from the humble letterhead or social media template to the dense annual review and advanced e-commerce platform. We strive for adaptability in a wide array of contexts. And with the ubiquity of mobile devices, we must consider how typography looks on various screen sizes and resolutions. Moreover, we have to think through accessibility and legibility for those with visual impairments.

By employing different typefaces, sizes, weights, colors, and spacing, we create a practice for headings, subheadings, and body text to organize information and emphasize the most important of elements. Ultimately, we have two mission objectives: to facilitate any and all communication from the brand and to provide a serviceable, yet distinct visual system. We are responsible for making both the lives of our clients easier and creating something beautiful that fosters connections with their communities.

"Readers usually ignore the typographic interface, gliding comfortably along literacy's habitual groove," writes Ellen Lupton in the pages of *Thinking with Type,* a masterful resource for designers. "Sometimes, however, the interface should be allowed to fail. By making itself evident, typography can illuminate the construction and identity of a page, screen, place, or product." At the end of the day, typography unites image and language. It is, in many ways, our glue.

Dinamo

Talking All Things Type Foundry

Dinamo Editions released *The Arizona Type Specimen*, a five-color, split-page, and spiral-bound publication designed by Hanzer Liccini, in celebration of ABC Arizona, the first ever sans-to-serif variable font to package its five looks into a single file.

Visited the luxury online retailer SSENSE lately? Acquired a bottle of Kendall Jenner's 818 tequila? Rolled a Rimowa suitcase through the airport? Popped over to Alicia Keys's website and digital archive? Joined a Discord chat group? If there is any question about typography's influence—its ability to sway what we think, feel, and do—a quick survey of Dinamo's work can provide the answers.

The type foundry's origin story begins in 2013 ("-ish," clarify its founders), when the German-Chilean designer Johannes Breyer teamed up with Swiss designer Fabian Harb. The duo began experimenting with typeface sketches, necessary components of their independent projects that slowly circulated among friends and gradually beyond. Two years later, they officially conspired to open their type studio despite no formal training in the subject. "We're self-taught," explains Breyer, "which has liberated us from some of the constraints and expectations elsewhere in our field."

Take the references that they look to. "We admire what Phoebe Waller-Bridge did with *Fleabag*," Breyer says. "She developed this relatable story. It's ironic, self-referential, and doesn't take itself too seriously. But it's

1 — SPREAD FROM *THE ARIZONA TYPE SPECIMEN*, AN ODE TO THE TYPEFACE DESIGNED BY ELIAS HANZER FOR DINAMO

Walter Alte Rauchwaren

Walter Alte Normalgrotesk

Walter Alte Röntgentherapie

Walter Neue Leicht
Walter Neue *Mager*
Walter Neue Normal
Walter Neue *Mittel*
Walter Neue Halbfett
Walter Neue Fett
Walter Neue *Extrafett*

2

Discord

3

Dinamo works to strike a balance
between self-initiated projects,
where they have full creative control,
and commissions, where they engage
in dialogue and problem solving.

also very complex and beautiful." Breyer and Harb hope to apply those same characteristics—familiarity and comfort juxtaposed with quirkiness and idiosyncrasy—to their fonts' universe. The ABC Walter typeface, for example, began as a research initiative exploring the Swiss designer Walter Käch's tool for teaching letterforms to students in the 1940s. Dinamo's analysis resulted in a twin family, which they liken to two related people "who get into all sorts of weird situations and help each other out." The firm draws cartoons for each style, Alte and Neue, to bring this story to life and even involves their followers with a monthly caption contest on Instagram and in their newsletter.

When it comes to brands, the Dinamo team firmly believes that typefaces serve as their voice. Through letters and execution, they capture their aspirations. When the atelier was tasked with crafting a logotype for Pharrell Williams's digital-first auction house Joopiter as part of the creative studio Alaska Alaska's identity design, Dinamo sharpened the forms of its own ABC Monument Grotesk typeface. Paired with the Joopiter's second, more ornamental logo, the wordmarks speak directly to both the digital and luxury sensibilities of the company. According to the Dinamo founders, typography should feel expressive but should never overpower other design elements. "Unless overpowering is the point," Breyer muses with a laugh, "in which case I would say, 'Let's go!'"

To partner with design studios or brands, Breyer, Harb, and the Dinamo team plunge in, first and foremost, with research and conversation. Getting to know one another is key. "You learn a lot about different worlds from your collaborators," they say. "And then together, you try to find a visual language in the shape of type that reflects their particular domain." Sometimes, the answer is tweaking characters from one of Dinamo's existing fonts, generating a solution that is distinctive and ownable but achieved within a healthy timeline and budget. Other times, a client's ambitions prove so specific and unique that they cannot be represented by something on the shelf, bringing bespoke typefaces into play.

When working with Commission Studio for the iconic luggage maker Rimowa, the Dinamo team made a site visit to the company's archive. They produced a typeface that combined neat detailing with small imperfections, an ode to the manufacturer's mechanic and hand-tooled processes. Later approached by Studio Koto for Discord, Dinamo dove headfirst into the gaming spaces that launched the platform. Pulling from historical references, it conceived of a customization of ABC Ginto, "an exuberant, geometric-humanist typeface that delights in tension." They attribute the success of both projects to the considerable time dedicated to discussion, exploration, and experimentation.

Certain endeavors, however, simply require more effort. Some brands, they say, necessitate "a toolbox that

2 — VARIATIONS WITHIN THE ABC WALTER TYPEFACE
FAMILY DESIGNED BY DINAMO AND OMNIGROUP
3 — WORDMARK DESIGN FOR DISCORD

allows them to dress in a way that's well suited to any occasion"—like when they set out to devise a moving, dynamic typeface that responds to sound for the San Francisco Symphony. In this case, they pursued a variable font. "Variable options let brands respond to shifts in technology and culture without having to change their entire wardrobe," Breyer elaborates. "The way this one stretches and flexes visually represents the dynamic and interactive nature of the institution."

Meanwhile, the International Olympic Committee, an organization that is incredibly large and far-reaching, needed a solution that communicates a variety of messages in a neutral way. Looking to fashion something equally laid-back and elegant, Dinamo created two typefaces, a related sans and serif. "Having both allows their designers not to get stuck in one tone of voice," says Breyer.

When asked what he loves most about his job, the agency's co-founder doesn't blink an eye. It all comes down to the diverse group of collaborators that he gets to partner with. "We have found ourselves in a situation," Breyer reflects, "where we can take something we find interesting—type—and apply it to so many different areas of production, from writing and design to technology and objects." The Dinamo practice, he continues, feels more like a way of thinking than a clear-cut process.

Though technically based in Berlin, Dinamo's studio operates through a network of satellite members across the globe. It currently consists of over a dozen young and energetic team players who are interested in how the world is changing at large. Type becomes their playground to explore its opportunities and its challenges. The emphasis, however, is on the word "playground." Of course, the Dinamo team takes their work seriously—just never too seriously. "We try not to fetishize what we do," Breyer says. "We hang out with friends. We go to shows. We stay in touch with the things that excite us most." And by doing so, they themselves continue to build one of the most exciting type foundries in the game.

4 — CUSTOMIZED TYPEFACE FOR SSENSE
5 — BESPOKE TYPE FOR TUMBLR
6 — ADAPTED TYPEFACE FOR LONDON'S ICA WITH
       IDENTITY DIRECTION BY CHRIS CHAPMAN

83

The brand consultancy Collins created a new identity for
the San Francisco Symphony, which included a partnership with
Dinamo. The San Francisco and New York-based firm invited
the type design studio to create a responsive font based on its
typeface ABC Arizona. In partnership, the two agencies developed
an internal and public-facing variable typographic tool that
dynamically responds in real-time to sounds, voices, and music.

7

8

AN UPDATED SAN FRANCISCO SYMPHONY
IDENTITY IN PARTNERSHIP WITH COLLINS

7 — CUSTOM TYPEFACE FOR THE SAN FRANCISCO SYMPHONY
8 — SAN FRANCISCO SYMPONY LOGO
9 — TYPE DESIGN FOR THE SAN FRANCISCO SYMPHONY

HEADQUARTERED IN ZAGREB,
STUDIO8585 IS THE PRODUCT OF MARIO
DEPICOLZUANE AND BENJA PAVLIN

Studio8585

With a career born from humble beginnings, Mario Depicolzuane found his first solo clients—his dentist, a former guitar teacher turned photographer, and a local real estate company—on his native island Krk, Croatia. Coming from his one and only agency job at Zagreb's Bunch, where he learned and developed international sensibilities from the company's creative director Denis Kovač, Depicolzuane formed Studio8585 in 2013 and manifested his very own dream job. Even if only working for local businesses and acquaintances, he was crafting something for the world. Depicolzuane now has a global client list, but he still thinks of them like his neighbors down the road, creating an intimate, close-knit community one collaborator at a time.

1

2

3

You have a very small team. How does your size benefit the identity development process? Studio8585 is composed of a core team of two, senior designer Benja Pavlin and me. We recently added a junior designer, and I'm considering looking for someone to fill an administrative role. Our size is deliberate. As a leader, I prefer smaller organizations with an intimate, human-forward approach. I want fewer meetings, less management, and more flexibility, freedom, and personal responsibility. There is only so much work that we can take on, but that restriction concentrates our offering and allows us to be picky, only working with clients who we think are a good fit. Because of our limited capacity, we can truly dedicate ourselves to the brands we work with. There's still a sense of structure and professionalism but also an increased openness. I consider brand work an ongoing conversation, which requires both sides to be fully involved.

I like to think of our studio as an artisanal restaurant or bar. We aren't necessarily focused on fine dining, but we have similar core principles: respecting and honoring the guests, the ingredients, and the process. We aim to make the experience, from the first email to a social media campaign 10 years later, as enjoyable as possible. Our studio is guided by a famous line from the American author Zig Ziglar: "Don't become a wandering generality. Be a meaningful specific." I think that by choosing to be small, we are setting ourselves up to be just that.

Speaking of ingredients, what is the most important component in any client-studio relationship? Trust. I can't say it enough. It is both given and earned. It must be mutual, and it develops over time. Because of our positioning, most brands who approach us are at least partially enrolled in our way of thinking and creating, so there's always an initial base to build on. In some cases, we lead the process in its entirety, and clients join us for the ride. In others, especially if the client comes from a creative industry, there is more nitty-gritty involvement.

I already had a strong relationship with Kinfolk's co-founder Nathan Williams from my time working there when he tapped me to conceive the original branding for The Audo, a hybrid space in Copenhagen comprising a hotel, a design showroom, a cafe, a restaurant, and a shop. We trusted each other, but simultaneously, because of his experience as a creative director, he knew exactly when and where to push us further. With certain elements of surprise, our work proved particularly impactful.

1 — PRINT APPLICATIONS FOR ARCHITECTURE OFFICE MVA
2 — ART DIRECTION FOR KINFOLK
3 — BRAND IDENTITY FOR ICONS BY MENU

4

5   6

TYPOGRAPHY—For The Audo, a hybrid space in Copenhagen,
the Studio8585 team settled on a contemporary yet organic
system built around the typeface Garibaldi. Complemented by
a bold and modern color palette, the typographic suite extends
across packaging, signage, and digital collateral.

4 — ORIGINAL BRAND IDENTITY FOR THE AUDO
5 — TYPOGRAPHIC PAPER CUPS FOR THE AUDO
6 — PUBLICATION DESIGN FOR CREATIVE VOYAGE PAPER

7   8

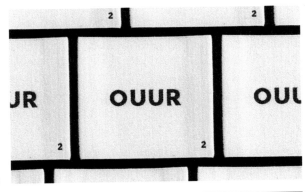

9

10

Timelessness and minimalism often go hand in hand. How do you leave room for playfulness in brand identities that have a more clean, thoughtful presence? Our foundation is rooted in the timeless, minimal, and conceptual approach established in the last century with the first modern corporate identities. A lot of our work sits on the shoulders of these very designs. Simultaneously, brands today have very different needs than in the 1960s or 1970s—or even the early 2000s. Our core elements, like a monogram or typography suite, tend to be conservative and practical. We then build on that primary layer with other components like illustration, photography, animation, or physical collateral, creating something dynamic and reflective of today—and hopefully tomorrow.

We recently finalized an identity for Clemente, a Los Angeles-based clinical research company working to advance healthcare by providing quality medical services for all, including underserved local communities. Their mission necessitates a clean and professional solution, but at the same time, they're looking to be different— more transparent, authentic, and human-centric—so we wanted their look to be sincere and approachable. We designed a bespoke typeface that we used in the wordmark, some display applications like titles and pull quotes, and in some more abstract, playful ways, where we isolated individual letters or combinations. Their main palette of black, white, and dark green reads pretty corporate, but when it feels right, we complement those colors with a warmer, secondary palette, too.

With inspiration at every corner, what drives your work? A natural curiosity helps my practice tremendously. As you develop as a designer or art director, you become an encyclopedia of references. A novel or album can be impactful, but visual resources are our bread and butter. I'm always collecting. I use the "save" function on Instagram. I take photos of everything that even remotely interests me and am constantly capturing vernacular type. I compile notes in Evernote. I have so many digital folders—old projects, previous explorations, inspiration for future, unknown endeavors.

Of course, I appreciate printed matter. I dive into thrift shops, antique bookstores, and occasionally libraries. I have piles and piles of books, catalogs, magazines, and record covers. These things ensure that my sources are broader and less fad-based. So much fantastic work has been created through the decades, across countries and fields. I try to stay open to that randomness, to maintain a fresh outlook with more depth and appeal than what's trending on social media.

A trip to Portugal a few years ago was particularly formative for me. I was digging through 50-year-old gallery catalogs in a secondhand bookshop and became

1   12

13

14

inspired by the intricate typography, design details, and simply the quality of the print production. These catalogs directly inspired a publication, *Creative Voyage Paper,* for the educational platform that I run. But they also encouraged me to be more proactive when it comes to digging. Much of what I find impacts my work, emboldening me to add more tactility, more craft, a visual surprise, or sense of playfulness.

How do you balance your tendency towards typography with other crucial design elements? If we look at brand identity as a well-executed dish, I see typography as the core ingredient or the main building block. There is something so powerful about its ability to connect language and form, to communicate. It has become central to our approach.

But while we need protein, there are all of these other macro- and micronutrients that make their way onto the "plate." We can't forget to add spice. Identities need to be clear and effective, but they also need to surprise and delight. Illustration can be an amazing tool. Photography is almost always indispensable. Design, meanwhile, is the art of putting these things together—it's the cooking and the plating. There is almost always something at the heart of the dish, but its success comes from taking all of these elements and finding a balance. Shifting their importance and looking at different ways to execute them gives us designers a very inspiring universe to work in, and enables us to find unique, visual stories for our clients.

11 — ALIUM GALLERY SIGNAGE
12 — VISUAL IDENTITY FOR ALIUM
13 — ALIUM PACKAGING
14 — BRAND CARD FOR ALIUM

STUDIO
PENTAGRAM

CLIENT
THE CONRAN SHOP

YEAR
2023

Sascha Lobe/Pentagram
The Conran Shop

CREATIVE DIRECTION
SASCHA LOBE
KIMBERLY LLOYD

ART DIRECTION
SASCHA LOBE
KIMBERLY LLOYD

PACKAGING AND
PRODUCT DEVELOPMENT
KIMBERLY LLOYD

Years before he began to call London home, Sascha Lobe visited The Conran Shop on trips to the city. "It was a must-visit stop," the Pentagram partner recalls, and one that would prove formative for his work on the visual overhaul of this contemporary design destination in conjunction with its 50th anniversary. In tandem with the brand strategist Kimberly Lloyd and The Conran Shop's chief executive Peter Jenkins, Lobe sought an open, diverse, and adaptable refresh reflecting the company's evolution, with changes including a new flagship store and pending expansion into the Middle East. Lobe, Lloyd, and Jenkins proceeded to develop an identity system that marries a modern, future-forward sensibility with hallmarks of the company's past.

Sir Terence Orby Conran, the designer, restaurateur, and retail magnate who founded the eponymous shop in 1973, died in 2020 at the age of 88. For all parties involved in the shop's refresh, it therefore felt apt to pay homage to Conran's enduring impact. "He has been our biggest source of inspiration," Lobe affirms. "We had a genuine conversation on his legacy—how he sought for the new, how he curated and selected." The designer went on to translate those notions into a logo system and bespoke typeface family, creating the building blocks for a versatile visual identity to be used as a universal language across the company's markets in the likes of London, Paris, Tokyo, and Seoul.

The Conran Shop Legacy Typeface Collection, which is the heart of the redesign, is markedly Bauhaus-inspired. Having updated the identity for the Bauhaus Archive, Lobe collaborated with The Conran Shop's Chelsea outpost in 2019 to celebrate the centennial anniversary of the influential art and design school. With a shared appreciation for all things Bauhaus, it makes sense, then, that Lobe would infuse its typographic principles into his designs for the brand. With each stroke and curve, Lobe set out to "mirror Sir Conran's discerning eye, his ability to create harmonious compositions."

With the typeface family established, the remaining assets fell harmoniously into place. The result, Lobe says, is a visual scheme that "exemplifies the brand's unwavering dedication to progress, design, and excellence" and in equal importance, "the visionary spirit of the brand's late founder."

POSTER DEPICTING VARIATIONS OF
THE CONRAN SHOP LEGACY TYPEFACE
COLLECTION

DISCOVERY —During celebrations for the 100th anniversary of Bauhaus in 2019, Lobe met Sir Terence Conran for the first time, an encounter that would shape his vision for The Conran Shop's refresh. "Seeing his relentless passion for design up close was truly invigorating," recalls Lobe.

THE OVERHAULED IDENTITY EXEMPLIFIES THE RETAILER'S DEDICATION TO THE ONGOING DEVELOPMENT OF DESIGN

T C S .

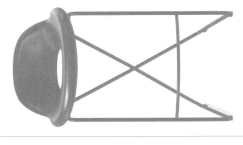

24pt

36pt

60pt

72pt

114pt

150pt

200pt

Latin Uppercase

Letter M

TCS Legacy Display
Typeface Cut

Regular
Typeface Weight

PHYSICAL—Playing with textures, high-gloss and matte finishes, touches like embossing, and a moody color palette of black, blue, and gray, brand strategist and Lobe's collaborator Kimberly Lloyd devised a diverse and layered packaging suite for The Conran Shop's relaunch.

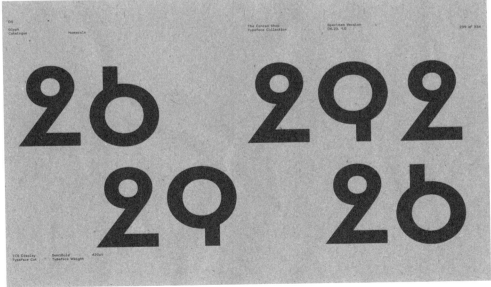

THE REFRESH PROVIDES A DIVERSE
AND FLUID VISUAL LANGUAGE

T C S .
T C S .

STUDIO
ATELIER DYAKOVA

CLIENT
MAD ET LEN

YEAR
2022

Atelier Dyakova
MAD et LEN

CREATIVE DIRECTION
SONYA DYAKOVA

GRAPHIC DESIGN
SONYA DYAKOVA

GABRIELLA VOYIAS
TOM BABER

TYPE DESIGN DIRECTION
GABRIELLA VOYIAS

TYPE DESIGN
TOM BABER
JAMES GRIFFIN

PHOTOGRAPHY
MATTEO CARCELLI
GUILLAUME ROUJAS

When creating a new identity for French artisanal scent makers Mad et Len, Atelier Dyakova sought to evoke the same tactile mood as the brand's products. "Each detail was beautifully crafted to immerse viewers in the company's surreal world," says Sonya Dyakova. She recalls diving into that very world with her team, noting that the process was made all the easier since the brand itself, as well as the majestic sculptural containers and poetic descriptions that house its products, was already rich with ideas.

Formed by Alexandre Piffaut and Sandra Fuzier in southern France, Mad et Len, as Dyakova learned, was born from the duo's travels to places like Africa, New Caledonia, the Fiji Islands, and Malaysia.

Despite these adventures, their main source of inspiration remains the rough terrain of the nearby Alps. "The complex scents evoke nature, raw materials, and a Proustian sense of longing," Dyakova suggests. With a deep appreciation for the French perfumer's principles, Atelier Dyakova created a visual identity to match. Drawing upon the enigmatic atmosphere of Mad et Len's headquarters, something of both a traditional apothecary and alchemist's lab, the studio went on to develop packaging, the logo, and a new website. The London team also helped lead art direction for the brand's photography suite.

For Dyakova, however, the heart of Mad et Len's new identity—as is the case

for many of the others she has helped conceive—lies in typography. The custom-designed typeface, its sharp and sculptural letterforms, is an amalgam of many things: the vernacular and hand-painted signage common to the south of France; the interiors and objects of traditional pharmacies; the black iron vessels that house Mad et Len's products, and Proust's famous autobiographical novel *À la recherche du temps perdu (In Search of Lost Time)*. Simultaneously, the typeface is also an ode to the artisanal craftsmanship infused in Mad et Len's scented candles, potpourris, and perfumes. "Typography," Dyakova says, "can express an expansive amount of character and reference, even in the smallest of details."

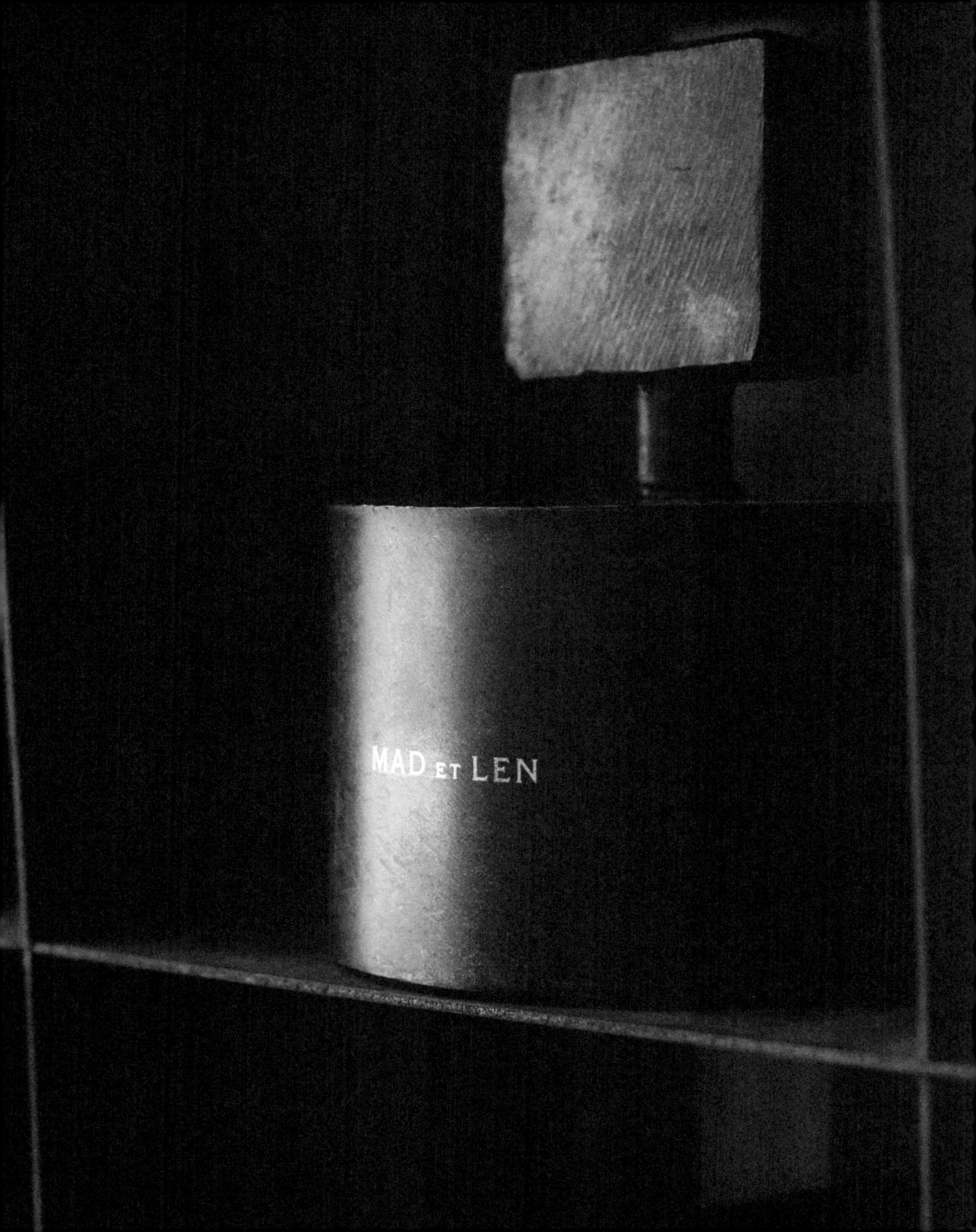
MAD ET LEN

PHYSICAL—To develop a packaging system, Atelier Dyakova employed tactile and engaging materials to achieve a careful balance of rough and smooth textures.

"For a brand that revolves around memory and feeling, physical touch and sense are crucial," says Dyakova.

M
& L

MAD ᴇᴛ LEN

MAKING OF BOIS D'ORAGE
AT MAD ET LEN ATELIER

DIRECTION—Through in-depth research, Dyakova developed a deep appreciation for the spirit of Mad et Len, which she and the studio team injected into its custom-drawn typography.

"We distilled the brand's essence into the letterforms, infusing everything that we then developed with a certain dark and alluring sensibility," she says.

A a € ;!*

A B C D E F G H I J K L M N O P Q
R S T U V W X Y Z 0 1 2 3 4 5 6 7 8 9

THÉ SICHUAN

CYPRÈS DE MAX

SPIRITUELLE

THE PACKAGING AND BESPOKE TYPE
EXUDE THE BRAND'S MOODY CHARACTER

Beautifully art-directed images—at once sensitive, artistic, and poetic—take center stage on Mad et Len's website and create an immersive shopping experience for the customer.

IV

Illustration

From the Drawing Board

Introducing Line & Shape

The late, great graphic design guru Milton Glaser frequently mused on the outsized role of illustration through history. "Look at the paintings of Pompeii," he encourages in *The Education of an Illustrator*, "the Aboriginal wall paintings of Australia, the great frescoes of Italy, and you understand a moment of time and the belief systems of the population." Similarly, illustration has the power to express the essence of a brand, artfully combining form, function, and fantasy.

Developing a brand identity is much like putting a puzzle together. We have the honor and responsibility of finding the missing pieces. What happens when words aren't enough, or a typographic solution doesn't do the trick alone? Illustration has the power to abstract an idea. It provides room for interpretation and imagination, eliciting emotional and intellectual responses. In conveying complex concepts in a simple and engaging way, illustration can differentiate a brand from its competitors.

In the aforementioned turn-of-the-century book, Véronique Vienne reminds us of the close bond between design and illustration, recalling designers who have honed their illustration skills such as James Victore and Paula Scher, as well as illustrators who have ended up opening design studios such as Glaser, Mirko Ilić, and Seymour Chwast. This mutual respect and understanding, Vienne remarks, only benefits our field. "By joining forces, graphic designers and illustrators produce work that's more focused and visible," she concludes. In a world where we are ever-increasingly exposed to imagery and content, clear visibility is imperative.

Moreover, as the demand for thoughtfully communicated, clean-cut messaging grows, so too does the value of illustration. Succinct visuals that convey a brand's tone of voice and reflect its attitudes can be used in a multitude of ways, from animated videos to social media posts and print materials. A flexible and dynamic branding tool, illustrations can be customized for specific campaigns, events, and products. Illustrations can also comprise the logotype, either alone or in conjunction with typography and lettering. A proponent of simplicity, the renowned American illustrator-turned-designer Paul Rand encourages us to remember that a logo's role is to identify. "No amount of literal illustration will do what most people imagine it will do. This will only make identification more difficult and the 'message' more obscure," he writes in his 1993 book *Design, Form, and Chaos*. "A logo, primarily, says who, not what, and that is its function."

An illustration thus must not only be appealing but serve its intended purpose. As we search for the right solution, we constantly keep the brand's personality, values, and audience in mind. We should be stylistically consistent with the overall identity and avoid being overly trendy or whimsical. We want to maintain our timeless principles, so we pursue styles that feel fresh and contemporary but that remain relevant over time. Potentially, we employ an evergreen illustrative archetype that can function over years or decades, particularly if the illustration is used for the logotype or brand symbol itself. At the same time, we also work to meet our needs without over art-directing. We seek illustrators whose style fits the concept, and whose aesthetics and preferences align with our own. Doing so allows us to give our collaborator some artistic breathing room. On the *Creative Voyage Podcast*, illustrator Merijn Hos, whose clients include Iittala and Disney, insists that the best partnerships result from a healthy balance of creative freedom and clear direction. "I'm happiest when a client says, 'This is what we want you to do. But we're going to give you a lot of creative freedom because we're confident that you will come up with something cool within this framework,'" he said. When we allow for this give and take, the pieces of the puzzle tend to fit together better and our designs are most successful.

Elsewhere, Glaser claimed that "there are three responses to a piece of design—yes, no, and WOW! Wow is the one to aim for." Throughout the identity development process, we constantly ask ourselves how we can make a brand stand out in a crowded marketplace or how we can foster deeper connections with their audience. When done well, illustration can be the answer, the wow factor we're looking for.

Mario Hugo

*Igniting the Fire
with Illustration*

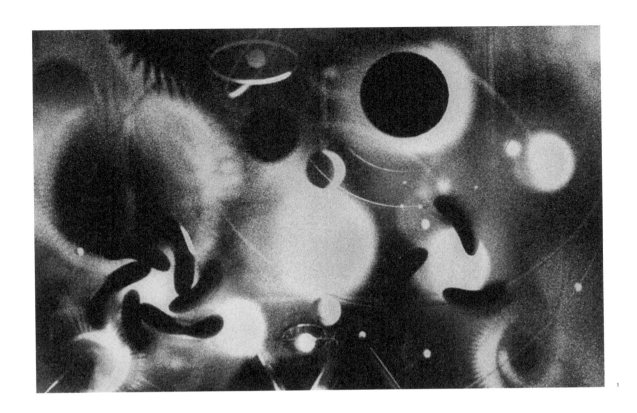

Hugo describes Odd One, an ongoing
and personal audio-visual project, as
a "petri dish." His otherworldly graphics
accompany music collaborations with
Golden Hum, Lord of the Isles, Mac Miller,
and Vince Staples, among others.

Mario Hugo recalls visiting his daughter's Waldorf school
years ago and confronting classrooms filled with faceless
wooden dolls. When he inquired about the figurines, he
was told that with a lack of eyes, ears, noses, and mouths,
the children could place their individual or imagined
spirits onto each one.

"I think that this is a meaningful analogy for the use
of anthropomorphic illustration by brands," Hugo says.
"It can be difficult to capture the inarticulable in pure
photography, and these are the cases where illustration
becomes particularly relevant."

A first-generation Argentinian-American, Hugo
grew up feeling othered, a sentiment that translated
to his creative pursuits. "I cut my teeth as a design-
minded illustrator," he recalls. "And I just had this early
ambivalence to agents." He and Jennifer Marie Gonzalez,
who he met when he moved to Brooklyn in 2004, had
a "silly idea" that transformed into an independent artist
management and creative agency of their own making, a
place where he could both give and receive support. Born in
2008, their eponymous studio Hugo & Marie began as a
"trial by fire," according to the artist-cum-agent.

2

3

The Precision Run campaign,
centered around a kinetic
manifesto film and illustrations
created by Jiro Bevis, aims to inspire
the brand's audience and convey
the emotional benefits of running.

2 — RADIATING LOGO FOR NIKE'S 2016 SUMMER
       OLYMPICS CAMPAIGN
3 — CREATIVE DIRECTION AND ILLUSTRATIONS
       FOR THE PRECISION RUN CAMPAIGN

"We were very young, very naive, and I have absolute
gratitude for our artists' trust in us."

Today, Hugo's client roster includes the likes of
Stella McCartney, Nike, Interscope Records, and 3.1
Phillip Lim. In other words, he interacts frequently with
brands, whether collaborating directly with his own
work or connecting other creatives for the job. "Brands
have the platforms to be radio towers and communication
satellites—to be beacons," he says. To him, they are much
more than a product, logo, or eye-catching color palette.
"They are the symphonies of all the frequencies they choose
to share with their audiences—and sometimes the ones that
they don't," he elaborates. "A brand's identity is the music
it plays, the honesty in its actor's voiceover, or the sing-song
alliteration in its written copy." He calls these elements
"subtle energies" that make up entire brand worlds. Many
times, in his eyes, these worlds are simply best inhabited by
one of his chosen art forms, illustration.

Above all, Hugo values transparency when working
with a brand. If the two have a mutual understanding of its
pain points and its audience, both parties are able to trust in
the process with greater ease. Hugo admits that he struggles
to recreate what his clients have in their imaginations, a
challenge that arises from his interest in new expressions
over house style. He likens his approach to experimenting
with chemicals in a bath or turning over rocks. "It is about
having the sensitivity to see something wonderful emerge
in those vague patterns," he muses.

Such exploration is key for ESP Institute, the Los
Angeles-based electronic music label that Hugo co-founded
with Andrew Hogge in 2010. As its creative director and
in-house artist, he constantly gets to ask one of his favorite
questions: "What does music look like?" He finds the
answers through illustrations and animations that mirror
its rich, experimental soundscapes and appear across album
covers and on merchandise.

With his rich knowledge of the industry and his
deeply embedded methods, Hugo has developed an agency
that is run by creatives for creatives. He attributes its success
to a common philosophy. "I think clients come to us for
a shared ethos, and we listen for that same ethos in our
collaborators," Hugo explains. "We tend to identify with
designers who think like illustrators and illustrators who
think like designers." After all, Hugo perceives everything
from strategy to tone of voice and copy to be a design
problem. The beauty then lies in "distilling communications
down to simple, elegant, and ineffable forms."

He reminisces on launching Precision Run, an indoor,
performance-based sub-brand from the luxury gym
company Equinox. "We viewed Precision Run as Equinox's
feisty younger sister," he says. And so he brought in the
London-based illustrator Jiro Bevis to create pulpy and
subversive figures including a sprinting cheetah, rabbit, and

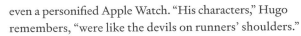

even a personified Apple Watch. "His characters," Hugo remembers, "were like the devils on runners' shoulders."

To produce work that best serves his clients' needs, Hugo listens to both them and his collaborators, which include talents such as Merijn Hos, Emma Larsson, and Moonassi, with the utmost attention. "We triangulate what is happening in ethers of culture, creativity, and in the lives of the consumer," Hugo says. "I hate the word 'consumer,' but I'm very attached to these three Cs." Hugo also avoids putting timelessness on a pedestal. Living in the present, he suggests, proves more important to generating great ideas, which inherently age well. He works from the heart, tells stories with empathy, and encourages those under his wing to do the same. "Style is invariably going out of style," he reminds them. "Don't borrow. Don't compare. Trust in yourselves and in your partners to create expressions that make the world more beautiful—not just more comfortable."

4

5

6

4 — PART OF LENNARD KOK'S SERIES *TRANSCENDENCE*
5 — WORK FOR NIKE BY LENNARD KOK
6 — ILLUSTRATION FROM ARTIST MERIJN HOS

Album artwork has fascinated Hugo since childhood, so it's unsurprising that his portfolio now includes covers for the likes of Rihanna, Beck, Alabama Shakes, and a slew of the artists on the label he co-founded with Andrew Hogge, ESP Institute.

THE VARYING FORMS
WITHIN HUGO'S WORK

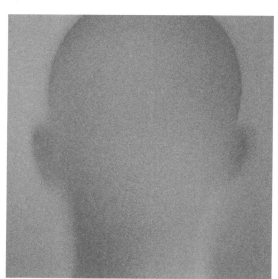

6

7

6 — A SERIES OF ALBUM COVERS DEVISED BY HUGO
7 — ART AND DIRECTION FOR SONNS & TAVISH
(ESP INSTITUTE)

SONYA DYAKOVA HELMS HER EPONYMOUS
STUDIO ATELIER DYAKOVA IN LONDON

Atelier Dyakova

Sonya Dyakova had long contemplated a studio of her own, but it wasn't until the birth of her daughter—the catalyst for leaving her full-time job as a design director at Phaidon Press—that Atelier Dyakova was born. Her studio's first project emerged after she sent an unsolicited email to the Fondation Cartier, resulting in a monograph on the Australia-born, London-based sculptor Ron Mueck. In her original workspace, a rented desk in the corner of another design firm with a window overlooking a construction site, she and a sole intern labored as hard and as fast as they could. Now heading up a small agency in a dedicated office, Atelier Dyakova has become a renowned entity in itself—although its founder still never shies away from a good old-fashioned cold call.

In brief, can you describe how you approach developing a brand identity from start to finish? Everything begins with a conversation. Meeting in person is always best and site visits are ideal, but it's possible to limit these interactions to telephone or video calls.

Through dialogue, we establish the project's requirements and identify the specific design challenges. Together, we answer some basic questions: Who are you? What do you want to say? What qualities do you want to portray? What is the purpose or mission of your brand? What are the unique characteristics of the company? Who is your audience?

We look at the competition to understand how we can do better or be different. We build up research, looking for references that might lead to appropriate, meaningful, and story-forward solutions. We observe and compose critical ideas, teasing out particularities that can serve as vehicles for our graphic concepts.

We present our ideas in a proposal, listen to our client's feedback, refine further, and, bit by bit, approach the finish line. We carefully assemble the project, ensuring that we remain guardians of original thinking.

Years ago, before I started my own agency, I worked at design studio Kerr Noble where the motto was "Think a lot, do little." I recall this maxim often, and the philosophy is such a large part of our approach now. It sounds so obvious, but thinking paves the foundation for any great project.

What makes for a healthy client-studio relationship? We appreciate when a client trusts us and has the courage to create something unique. I say "courage" because it is challenging to be brave when so much is at stake. Our brains are designed to naturally gravitate towards the familiar.

There's something called the "mere-exposure effect," a phenomenon where we develop a preference for things simply because they are recognizable or because we're already accustomed to them. Our creative process really blossoms when a client shows a willingness to explore the unknown.

Real valuable feedback is necessary too. At times, businesses are prescriptive in their feedback, which can prove restrictive to creative thinking. If I could offer brands advice, I would say, "Avoid prescribing. Use constructive criticism instead." Together, studios and clients have to chip away to determine what is essential. A level of articulation leads to much better results.

1 — IDENTITY FOR HAUSER & WIRTH PUBLISHERS FEATURING TYPE MARK
2 — MONOGRAM FOR HAUSER & WIRTH PUBLISHERS

27 Oct – 4 Dec, 2020

EPFL HORIZOOM

SOMETIMES
DOING NOTHING
LEADS
TO SOMETHING

Talks, installations, screenings & workshops on the creative potential of a moment of nothingness

PHYSICAL — For the Lausanne-based cultural platform Archizoom, Atelier Dyakova created an expressive and flexible visual system to epitomize its curious and rebellious attitude. The studio opted for humble, lo-fi materials for its printed collateral to "reflect the irreverent do-it-yourself attitude of Archizoom Associati," a radical Italian design group established in 1966 and the organization's namesake.

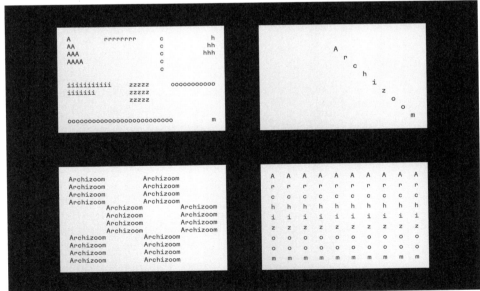

3 — POSTER CAMPAIGN FOR ARCHIZOOM EXHIBITION
4 — ARCHIZOOM STATIONERY ENVELOPE
5 — BUSINESS CARDS FOR ARCHIZOOM

6

7

8

6 — WEBSITE AND BRAND IDENTITY FOR NEIGHBOUR
7 — HANG TAGS FOR NEIGHBOUR
8 — SIGNAGE FOR NEIGHBOUR
9 — STICKER BEARING THE NEIGHBOUR LOGO

Are there any particular tools that have positively impacted your work? A £2.95 Muji pocket file with transparent A4-sized sleeves proved completely transformative for me. I learned to use it at one of my previous jobs. With this folder, I could slowly, piece by piece, construct my thoughts. I could build links and references or show relationships between images, words, and ideas. The fact that I could insert and remove stuff from the file enabled me to edit my thoughts. Now, I do the same thing but on my computer. I have a digital document where I can trace my ideas and determine if they have a leg to stand on.

How do you create visual identities that retain relevance over time? I try to avoid a cookie-cutter approach where the same elements are repeated over and over again. Consistency is indeed essential in branding. However, it can start to feel a little flat if the creative work is not evolving. Building a brand identity is like composing a soundtrack for a film. You must find ways to touch on the same themes, while still introducing variations and inventive ways to create an atmosphere—in our case, the rich universe of a brand.

Do you ever implement surprise touches, like illustration, to achieve that variety? Of course. Illustration, and other elements like photography, can enrich the visual language of an identity. With the Vancouver-based shop Neighbour, we set out to put their gentle and warm approach to curating clothing and objects at the center of their identity. We commissioned the British artist Hatty Staniforth to create a captivating identity infused with a human touch, contrasting the ultra-contemporary typeface that we had selected. Hatty's drawings carry a poetic quality that is personal, timeless, revered, and full of humor—they instill the brand with a sensitivity that speaks to community. In this case, illustration brought in a sense of storytelling, creating energy and making other elements like the sans-serif type come alive.

You say that your approach is rooted in typographic experimentation. Where did your interest in type develop? In many ways, I was drawn to typography by accident. I heard a few people remarking on my skills throughout school and just after graduating. In a way, it gave me a boost of confidence. If you have a skill, use it.

On the other hand, my interest in type dates back to my childhood. My family lived in a small Soviet apartment, and while my parents were busy working as architects, I spent a lot of time with my grandmother. She was an art teacher and created costumes and masks for stage productions. She also did hand-lettering for youth theater posters. It's in this environment that I nurtured

9

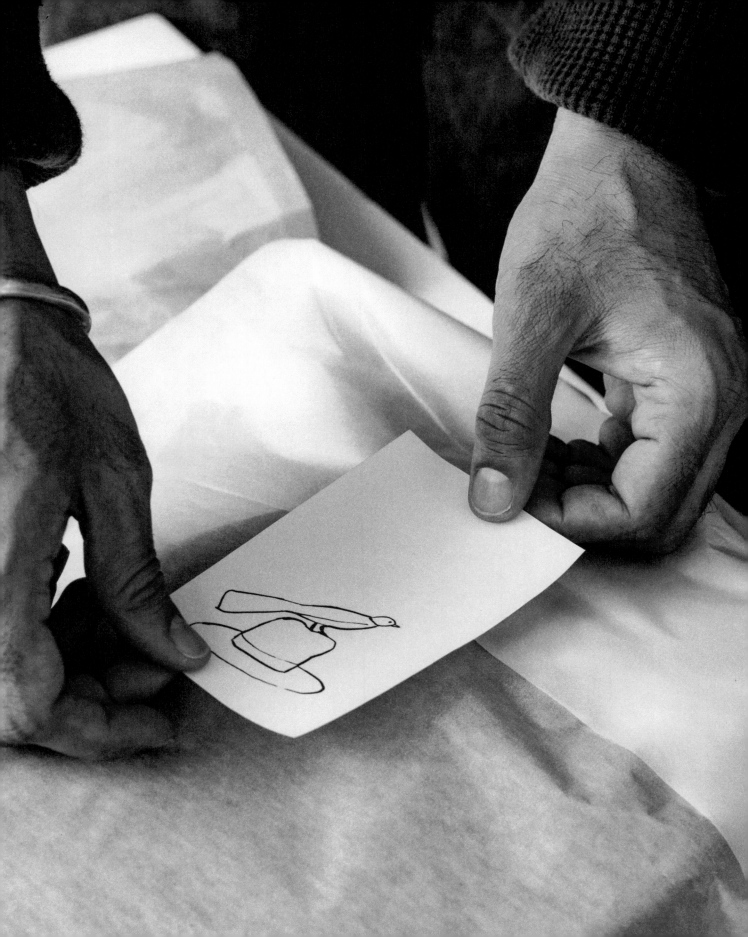

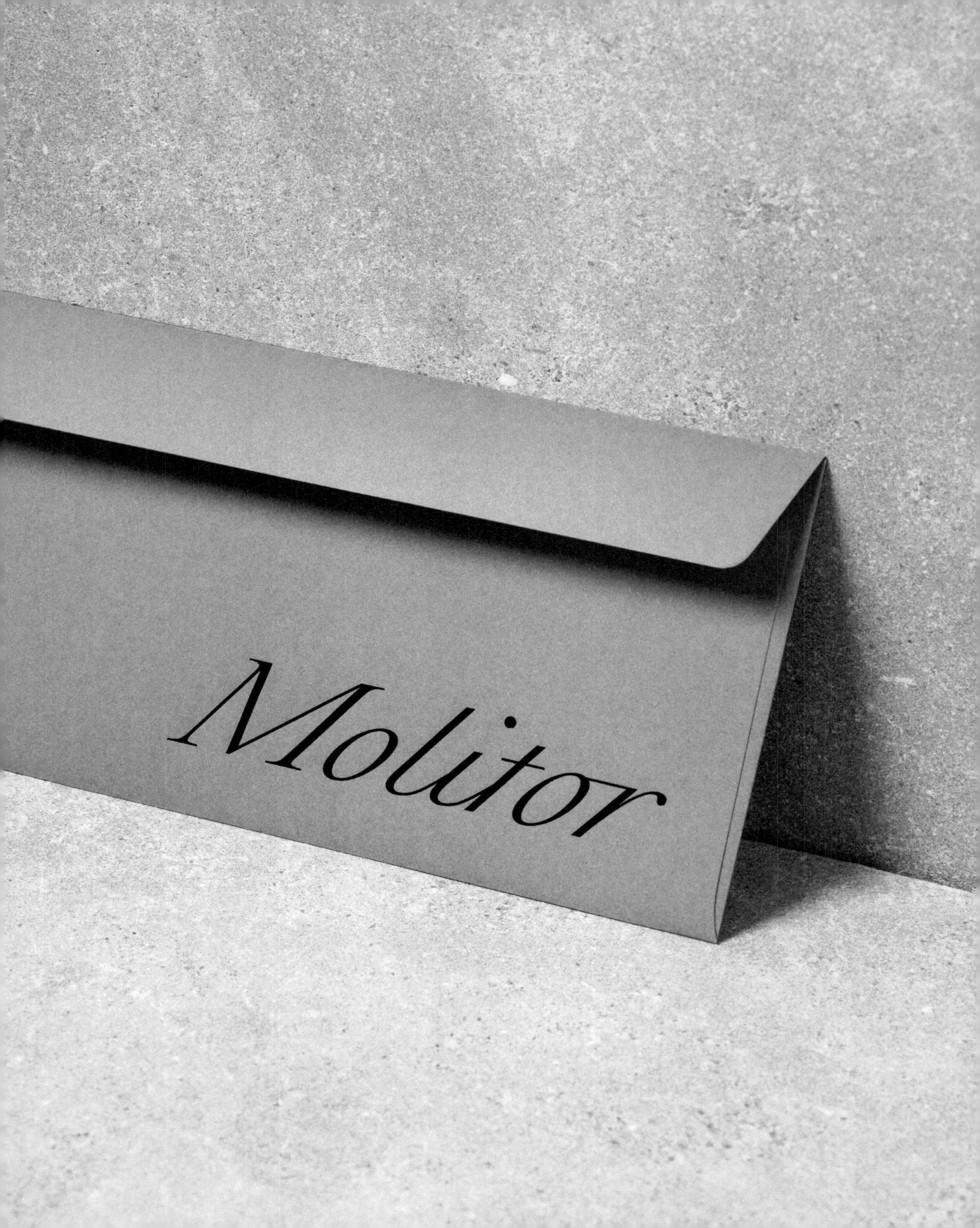
Molitor

11

my love for typography. I *so* enjoy exploring its potential. It can be playful or serious. It's a great communication tool. I am also open to type taking a back seat, allowing other elements, like images or color, to take over. I like creating various compositions using different ratios of ingredients. I don't see typography as more significant than photography, illustration, or layout. A successful brand identity considers all components with equal care and attention. Everything finds its place and role, ultimately working together in unison.

12

13

STUDIO
BIELKE&YANG

CLIENT
HELSEUTVALGET

YEAR
2016

(GAY AND LESBIAN
HEALTH NORWAY)

Bielke&Yang
Helseutvalget

ART DIRECTION
MARTIN YANG
CHRISTIAN BIELKE

GRAPHIC DESIGN
EVAN MCGUINNESS

PHOTOGRAPHY
KIMM SAATVEDT

PROJECT MANAGEMENT
AKSEL OVERSKOTT

ILLUSTRATION
HEDOF

WEB DEVELOPMENT
VÆRSÅGOD

When the Norwegian LGBTQIA+ sexual health organization Helseutvalget revealed its new brand identity in 2017, the results were immediate. Conceived by Bielke&Yang, the refresh doubled website traffic and significantly increased the number of people making contact via online chat, text message, and email. Consequently, the redesign helped Helseutvalget expand its outreach. "More than 1,000 HIV tests were ordered in the first few days after the launch alone," recall the studio's founders Christian Bielke and Martin Yang.

Prior to this update, Helseutvalget employed individual identities for each of its projects, which it now sought to unify in an effort to better clarify its messaging. The logo, consisting of two figures embracing to form the letter H for "Helseutvalget," expresses care and health. These soft shapes and bright yet reserved color palette are implemented consistently throughout the organization's entire identity—on tote bags, in reading materials, on T-shirts, and even on their free condoms. According to Bielke and Yang, they conceived this welcoming aesthetic to encourage people to contact Helseutvalget. "The use of illustration adds a certain playfulness and acts to disarm content that might find people during very vulnerable situations," they suggest.

The Bielke&Yang team created a look and feel that would reach those who do not necessarily identify openly as LGBTQIA+, or who might simply be uncomfortable with ordering an HIV test kit. "Inclusive" and "friendly" therefore became key words in considering design solutions. Working closely with Hedof, the one-man studio helmed by Dutch illustrator Rick Berkelmans, the Norwegian agency endeavored to provide Helseutvalget with a comprehensive and good-natured image. These illustrations, in combination with photographs from the likes of Kimm Saatvedt, make potentially intimidating resources such as websites and booklets less imposing and easier to access.

"This new visual identity has enabled Helseutvalget to effectively communicate its mission and services to a broader audience," say Bielke and Yang. "And it has helped the organization to establish a more approachable and inviting image, while maintaining a professional and trustworthy appearance."

TYPOGRAPHY—To balance the logo's softer forms, Bielke&Yang decided on a legible, clean-cut typeface that retains a sense of friendliness while conveying reliability and experience.

Helseutvalget

THE LOGO REFLECTS THE ORGANIZATION'S
COMMITMENT TO CREATING SAFE AND
SECURE SPACES

DIGITAL —Helseutvalget planned to join in on Norway's 2020 Pride celebrations, but when they were canceled due to the pandemic, Bielke&Yang proposed a different approach to celebrate love and diversity. With an extensive, animated illustration from Rick Berkelmans, an ersatz digital "parade" allowed participants to learn about the organization's offerings in a more lighthearted way.

Rick Berkelmans's illustrations bolster the company's approachability.

A BUSINESS CARD FOR HELSEUTVALGET
BEARS THE WORDMARK AND LOGO

PHOTOGRAPHY — In partnership with Ferdi Film, Bielke&Yang produced and directed a campaign featuring volunteer models who share their personal attitudes towards sexual health and wellness. Set on a pink couch and shot in natural light, the imagery maintains the approachable sensibility that the studio worked to infuse across Helseutvalget's assets.

PHYSICAL COLLATERAL, WHETHER A
WATER BOTTLE OR PAMPHLET, IS DEFINED
BY THE HELSEUTVALGET COLOR PALETTE

STUDIO	CLIENT	YEAR
FNT	ONJIUM	2021

Studio FNT
ONHARU

CREATIVE DIRECTION	ART DIRECTION
HEESUN KIM	WOOGYUNG GEEL

GRAPHIC DESIGN	WEBSITE DESIGN
YOUJEONG LEE	YOUJEONG LEE

Best known for its Michelin-starred restaurant offering up elegant, seasonal fare, Onjium, a Seoul-based research institute for traditional Korean culture, wears many hats. This multiplicity was well understood by Studio FNT when they were asked to usher in the visual identity for two new projects under the Onjium umbrella. Adhering to the client's mission of "restoring the legacy of the past while building bridges to the future," as articulated by Jaemin Lee, Heesun Kim, and Woogyung Geel, the Studio FNT team was tasked with bolstering the Onjium brand while developing an identity for something altogether new.

As part of this brief, Onjium's research institute arm was seeking to resurrect ancient Korean textile patterns, bringing them into the public eye with a contemporary bent. They had chosen four configurations, dating from the 14th to

19th centuries, to represent the seasons. Studio FNT subsequently digitized each one with updated color combinations, printing them via silkscreen onto *hanji* paper. The team then capitalized on the flexible nature of the designs, translating them across a number of products including envelopes, fans, and toilet paper holders. Deliberately de-emphasizing the brand name across the product line allows the prints, with their inherent worth and beauty, to speak for themselves.

Then, in the midst of the Covid-19 pandemic, Onjium launched Onharu, an offshoot brand with a more relaxed persona stocking various domestic goods. While food is the platform's main component, it also provides table linens and other homewares to encourage more holistic gathering experiences. Studio FNT maintained several elements from

the patterns project, translating them onto textiles and print collateral within the soft Onharu color palette. Within the logotype, convex glyphs reflect the brand's bountiful nature. The geometric illustrations are full and rounded, conveying, according to Lee, Kim, and Geel, "a sense of generosity and abundance." These storytelling elements are metaphors for the areas of food, clothing, and housing that define Onjium at large. In Korean, *onjium* means "to make with integrity," and the co-founders say that components like illustration allow the team to thoughtfully communicate their message.

The relationship between the institute and Studio FNT is one of a shared ethos, where both parties seamlessly work toward the same desired end. "When we have been learning about a brand for such a long time and, like an artist, get to paint their portrait," says the trio, "it's the kind of work that we really love."

ONHARU

ONHARU

THE ILLUSTRATIVE ONHARU
LOGO AND WORDMARK

DIRECTION—Inspired by Joseon, the last dynastic kingdom of
Korea, and the clothes of its noble families, the FNT team employed
a color palette that includes jade green, pale brown, and white.

Photography

Photo Finish

Crafting
Visual Narratives

The best-selling U. S. author and so-called "king of marketing" Seth Godin claims that content marketing is the only type of marketing we have left. What's more, he's right: content rules all. Yes, we need an impressive logo, typeface system, and color palette, but at the end of the day, a brand continuously frames and reframes itself around its content. In the age of the internet, where much of what we encounter is visual, photography—whether in the form of still images or film—is an invaluable instrument in our figurative toolbox.

On a purely functional level, photography can showcase a brand's products or services. Simultaneously, however, it can create a sense of trust and authenticity, tell a story, convey a mood, or evoke emotions. It also has the potential to be the thing that keeps an audience captivated and committed. As stewards of brand identities, we are frequently tasked with shaping the look and feel of visual assets in order to achieve those more meaningful results.

"It is an illusion that photos are made with the camera," noted the master French photographer Henri Cartier-Bresson. "They are made with the eye, heart, and head." As brands increasingly cater to niche audiences on a competitive, often global market, his sentiment rings even truer today. We have the power to turn photography into one of the most relevant resources for the brands we help mold. As such, we must think carefully about our target demographics and produce material that will resonate and be both appropriate and remarkable.

There are, of course, innumerable styles and approaches. We might opt for something clean and minimalistic, or we might aim for a more real-life, effortless expression. We might even employ analog processes so to inspire a sense of intimacy or nostalgia. Regardless of the direction we choose to take, brand photography should always be well conceived, well executed, and visually engaging.

To build awareness and recognition, we develop a cohesive and recognizable identity, bolstered by these visuals. Our duty lies in ensuring that the brand's imagery is consistent with the other identity elements that we have implemented. Every visual component that we bring to the table should fit into a larger story. In addition to considering themes, location, and styling, as well as essentials like lighting and composition, we should also take the final retouch into account. Post-processing can be used to enhance the quality of the image and create the harmony that we strive for.

Our defining standards for static photography prove equally valuable when it comes to the moving image. Video content provides continued storytelling opportunities, but with the inclusion of music and sound design, it can connect with viewers on an even deeper level. If a photograph is indeed worth a thousand words, then a meticulously crafted brand film can be priceless.

Yet, to create any lasting impression, we must find the right collaborators. The team we choose directly influences the quality of our work. An art director is only as successful as his photographers, videographers, and stylists. We search out kindred spirits, those who are conceptually and philosophically aligned with our creative vision to bring it to life. We can direct—or even try to force—a specific outcome, but if the people in charge of producing it aren't the right fit, we won't succeed. This entire process is a dialogue. There must be space for discussion and interpretation from both sides. We choose our partners for their individual styles, and it's only fair that we respect their viewpoints—as we hope they do ours.

Together, we aim to inform and to move. We work to communicate the "why" of the brand, while aspiring to create eye-catching and attention-grabbing visuals. Alexey Brodovitch, the Russian-American art director and fashion photography icon, was early to notice that the public is oversaturated and, to put it more simply, tired. "The disease of our age is this boredom, and a good photographer must successfully fight it," he observed. "The only way to do this is by invention and by surprise." It is our job, then, to lead the charge.

Alexander Saladrigas

*Kicking Ideas around
with a Master Image-Maker*

1

When it comes to the power of photography, Alexander
Saladrigas doesn't mince his words. "It is one of the best
ways to convey a brand's identity," he says assertively.
"It can capture feelings, dreams, and attitudes, and if a brand
curates their photos well, it can provide people a clear
sense of belonging."

Born and raised in Miami, Florida, Saladrigas
embraced pen and paper as his first love. "Drawing was
an outlet," he remembers. "It gave me a place where I felt
like I fit in." But when he graduated from high school,
he purchased his first camera and discovered his soulmate.
It took several years for Saladrigas to establish his
refined style and to really learn the medium's potential.
"Photography," he came to understand, "is a reflection
of how you see the world, what you find beautiful, and
the moments that give you an impulse to capture them."
For this proud Cuban-American, the rest is history.

Now based in New York City, Saladrigas's work
explores the concepts of family and culture. He captures
fathers and sons for a series titled "Dads" that highlights
the different shapes fatherhood can take. Elsewhere, he
has also documented the lives of immigrant families in the

2

ISABEL MARANT

3

Saladrigas still maintains an analog practice, and he shot the Isabel Marant accessories campaign entirely on film. His imagery made its way to digital billboards in New York City and wheat-pasted posters across Paris.

United States for "The Land of Milk and Honey," a multi-artist project that describes itself as an "audit of the American dream." He has shot covers for editions of *Vogue* in Mexico and Ukraine, and his images have graced the pages of *New York Magazine, Harper's Bazaar,* and *The Cut.* Saladrigas, however, is also responsible for helping brands including Louis Vuitton, Isabel Marant, and haircare line Sándor craft their visual worlds, conveying intangible elements like their values and personality.

Regardless of the assignment at hand, Saladrigas comes to the table inspired. His work is profoundly influenced by everyday things like music, film, family, and above all, people—particularly those on the other side of his lens. "Taking someone's photo can be a moment of vulnerability, of openness, and connection," he explains. "I'm most inspired by sharing moments with individuals from all walks of life, by hearing their stories."

People, as it turns out, can also make or break a successful shoot. "It's very common to see a brand's team hire a talented photographer and then try to control every element," Saladrigas says. "In the end, this clouds the message and forces the artist to create work they're unfamiliar with, which tends to turn out badly." He pleads with brands to hire the right artist for the job and give that person creative freedom in turn—or in other words, not to commission someone to produce content that doesn't fit within their portfolio.

"I am lucky to work for brands that hire me for my vision," he acknowledges. "It is often a truly collaborative process." Typically, a brand's art director offers a mood board or a general concept as a starting point, and together, they refine the story from there. If Saladrigas isn't particularly familiar with the company or business, he does his due diligence and looks to previous campaigns and collections. This insight allows any remaining details like location, cast, and hair and makeup choices to fall easily into place. "Beyond the pre-production, a lot happens organically while I'm shooting," Saladrigas says. "I become immersed in the moment and the brand's world."

The result is work that resonates well beyond the photographer and production team. Take Nordstrom's popular spring 2021 campaign, where the retailer hired four photographers and gave them a succinct brief: make people feel good. Saladrigas was immediately reminded of simple childhood pleasures—playing a game, jumping on a trampoline, or throwing a ball around—and incorporated them into his indoor shoot. With the unlimited ability to choose who, what, and how he wanted to photograph, he produced a set of images that stand apart from run-of-the-mill fashion photos. "Each photographer interpreted the brand in their own way," recalls Saladrigas, who remarks that, despite the autonomy he was afforded, "it was interesting to see how all of the images still had a cohesive feeling."

Recently, Amazon Prime brought Saladrigas on to shoot promotional images for their coming-of-age series *The Summer I Turned Pretty.* Saladrigas joined the actors on the beach, as opposed to in the studio, where these shoots frequently take place. "They wanted someone who could be trusted to deliver images that felt young and fresh on location," he says. The Amazon team worked on post-production but kept in close contact with Saladrigas, who helped with color to ensure that the imagery stayed true to his aesthetic. Billboards with the final product appeared across cities like New York and Los Angeles, making their way to Instagram accounts, proving that, when a brand and photographer complement one another, the work speaks for itself.

Always faithful to his creative ideals, Saladrigas shoots photos that break through the noise. "We open our phones every day and are flooded with images," he says. "While we may barely think about something that we see, our brains are always labeling, organizing, and searching for familiarity." If we can find that familiarity in a brand, he continues, we develop trust and loyalty. When asked what his secret is, Saladrigas admits that it isn't so mysterious. "I try to bring an air of humor and humanity to my photos," he says. "I aim to create work that is unexpected and fantastical or simply vulnerable and real."

4

Saladrigas opted to shoot in natural settings for Sándor, a haircare company that emphasizes biodegradable ingredients and sustainable practices. His imagery is often overlaid with the brand's wordmark designed by the New-York based agency Ania et Lucie.

5

2 — IMAGERY FOR REBECCA TAYLOR FALL 2021
3 — ISABEL MARANT 2019 CAMPAIGN PHOTOGRAPHY
4 — SPRING 2021 WORK FOR NORDSTROM
5 — BRAND IMAGES FOR SÁNDOR

TRISTAN CEDDIA AND RICK MILOVANOVIC
RUN THE MELBOURNE-BASED GRAPHIC
DESIGN STUDIO TRIC

TRiC

The relationship between Tristan Ceddia and Rick Milovanovic is what some might call a slow burn. They were friends. They shared an office. They collaborated on projects. In fact, they even had a name for their collective force—TRiC, an acronym for "Tristan and Rick in Company" (initially spelled "TRICK" before the "K" on Milovanovic's keyboard went missing). After working separately for nearly two decades, Ceddia and Milovanovic formally joined forces in 2020—and thus their studio was born. Ever since, they have been picking up the pace, creating a positive working culture within their Melbourne atelier's walls while producing original, lasting work outside of them.

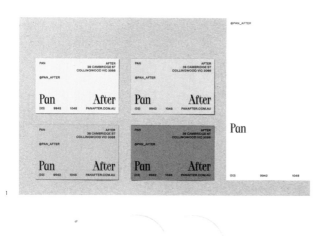

What have you discovered to be an unexpected but invaluable resource? Teaching has been such an important tool for us. We began a few years ago after being invited by our former lecturer and friend Warren Taylor, who now heads design at Melbourne's Monash University. He gave us individual briefs to teach and encouraged us to write our own brief—something that we would like to be taught ourselves—to teach together. The result was Everyday Messaging, which we offered to final year students between 2018 and 2021.

The two of us look to ideas from opposite ends of the spectrum. We keep the familiar both close and at arm's length. When things come easy, we push harder. Likewise, we encouraged students to stumble blindly through a very unconventional design process to discover the unexpected. We forced them to search outside of the design zeitgeist: no Instagram, no Pinterest, no preconception. Instead, they chose a topic made by a non-designer—for instance, matrix markings from construction workers—and then dove deep into research, interviews, and documentation. Through their learnings, they conceived new projects. Instead of starting with a solid idea in mind, they let the journey generate the outcome. The brief yielded a broad spectrum of results. Some work failed, and failure is essential. But other work succeeded, producing new experimental typefaces, children's toys, packaging systems, clothing ranges, video, photography, sculptures, and even a speculative variation on the English language.

We learned so much alongside our students. Our greatest gain, however, has been people—our first two employees at the studio, Chloe Papas and Marissa Hor, were top graduates, and carry the philosophy of Everyday Messaging through at TRiC.

How does that approach translate into your studio work? There's a quote from the American director J.C. Chandor's 2014 film *A Most Violent Year* where the protagonist Abel Morales, played by Oscar Isaac, says, "When it feels scary to jump, that is exactly when you jump. Otherwise you end up staying in the same place your whole life, and I can't do that." His words remind us to always push into new territories. Who knows how far we might fly? Where we might land? What we might find?

In our practice, we look at the walls, the ground, up in the sky. We look at literature, philosophy, politics, sports, old books, new books, magazines, punk zines, vernacular signage, design by non-designers, art, architecture, fashion. But most importantly, we look at the future.

1 — BUSINESS CARDS AND STATIONERY FOR PAN AFTER
2 — PROMOTIONAL COLLATERAL FOR WILDFLOWER
3 — BRAND ASSETS FOR OLAVER

Hazelnut

PLEASE RECYCLE

Hunted+ Gathered

5

Hazelnut

Dark Organic Chocolate
70% Cacao

net 45g

Dark Organic Chocolate

Hunted+Gathered

huntedandgathered.com.au

The TRiC team devised an identity for the custom tailor and clothier P. Johnson that draws upon the brand's commitment to simplicity, sustainability, and craft.

4

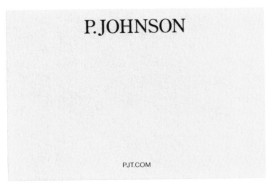

P.JOHNSON

PJT.COM

SYDNEY	MELBOURNE	NEW YORK	LONDON
7 Walker Ln	29 Thomas St	400 W Broadway	30 Percy St
Paddington	Windsor	New York	Fitzrovia

SYDNEY	MELBOURNE	TUSCANY	STUDIO
2 Chifley Sq	1 Crossley St	Via Martiri di Cefalonia	65 Oxford St
Sydney CBD	Melbourne CBD	MS Toscana	Paddington

5

7   6

For the bean-to-bar chocolate business Hunted+Gathered, TRiC developed a minimal, yet expressive visual system that takes cues from the likes of Kenya Hara, Dieter Rams, and Armin Hofmann.

4 — VISUAL CAMPAIGN FOR P. JOHNSON
5 — P. JOHNSON PHYSICAL COLLATERAL
6 — HUNTED+GATHERED STICKER DESIGN
7 — PACKAGING FOR HUNTED+GATHERED

We stretch things, turn them upside down, look at them backwards or through a microscope. We close our eyes, dream, travel, fight, run, ride, scribble, and struggle towards the work we produce.

The process can be more conventional, but more often than not, it isn't. We value our lens. We consider what we would love to see in the world without being guided by ego, arrogance, or overconfidence. We believe in inclusivity and do our best to devise messages that can be enjoyed by all. If we can make people smile, beginning with our clients, we know we're on the right path.

You lean towards the unconventional. Are there any clients who people might be surprised to learn are on your roster? The Human Rights Law Centre (HRLC), an Australian nonprofit organization. We took inspiration from the wonderfully reactive nature of passionate protest placards—always bold, always underlined. If there's a full stop, a marker more than likely snapped in the process. With this creative sentiment in mind, we embraced the organization's name to create a new logomark, leaning into the powerful words "human," "rights," and "law" to communicate: this is who we are, and this is what we do. Familiar language devices—the underline and full stop— eliminate hierarchy and emphasize each word equally. The resulting logomark is firm but friendly—confident, contemporary, and refined.

Instead of defaulting to traditional design studios that specialize in NGO branding, HRLC was drawn to the broadness of our work across different communities, organizations, and sectors. The very idea that they were willing to break away and approach a branding process with such foresight, to challenge the status quo of their industry, resonated with us. It's these kinds of client relationships—ones that cultivate new possibilities for design—that we dream of building.

Beyond words and graphics, how do you approach the process of translating a brand's essence and values into visual storytelling? We always present campaign direction as part of a project, even if it isn't a part of the initial brief. It is such a huge part of the way brands exist today, through social media, the internet, out-of-home communications. The client tends to really appreciate our direction. It helps to bring the project alive and give the brand a voice in its infancy. We usually visualize an overarching concept and art direction. We may suggest a photographer, location, or other essential elements to relay our vision and the importance of the campaign. We hate sending our babies—our brands—into the world without supporting visuals, so we see huge value in this process not only for us but for the brand and their audience.

8 — CLO STUDIOS BUSINESS CARD
9 — PROMOTIONAL MATERIAL FOR PAN AFTER
10 — STATIONERY FOR HUMAN RIGHTS LAW CENTRE

Hugh De Kretser
Executive Director

(03) 8636 4000
(03) 8636 4009

L17, 461 Bourke St   L5, 175 Liverpool St
Melbourne VIC 3000   Sydney NSW 2000   hrlc.org.au

Human
Rights
Law
Centre.

L17, 461 Bourke St   L5, 175 Liverpool St
Melbourne VIC 3000   Sydney NSW 2000

L17, 461 Bourke St   L5, 175 Liverpool St
Melbourne VIC 3000   Sydney NSW 2000

L17, 461 Bourke St   L5, 175 Liverpool St
Melbourne VIC 3000   Sydney NSW 2000

L17, 461 Bourke St   L5, 175 Liverpool St
Melbourne VIC 3000   Sydney NSW 2000

Human
Rights
Law
Centre.

Human
Rights
Law
Centre.

Human
Rights
Law
Centre.

TRiC conceived a custom wordmark, which they pair with Dinamo's Monument Grotesk Mono, for the Melbourne-based cheese merchant.

We recently developed an identity for the local cheese shop, Supercheese, where we created a custom typeface and utilized photography from our friend Lauren Bamford. The client loved how this brought the brand to life, quickly seeing the value in creating a campaign with Bamford in order to elevate the brand. Elements from the photoshoot made their way into the store design, website, social media, and a whole range of collateral—all aspects of the brand that would have otherwise been purely graphic.

When it comes to branding, where does the studio's job end and the client's begin? We of course aim for success with the brands that we create. We do our best to vet a project or client to ensure that they align with our own values as far as quality, ethics, and proposition. That said, we have no control over how a brand is marketed or presented, or whether a service is being provided adequately. Those tasks are up to the client. We know we can create amazing brands, but we have to leave it to them to ensure that the work hits the market in the right way. The metrics we employ start with the happiness of the client, and, if the company, product, or service is right, continue through to the happiness of the customer. Everyone can put on a fancy pair of shoes, but feeling comfortable and knowing how to move in the right direction is a different story.

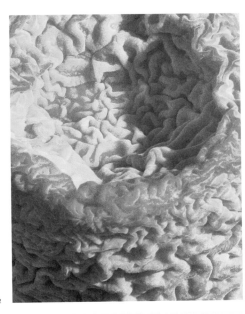

11   12

13

11 — ART DIRECTION FOR SUPERCHEESE
12 — DETAIL SHOT FOR SUPERCHEESE
13 — SUPERCHEESE PRODUCT PHOTOGRAPHY

STUDIO   CLIENT   YEAR
STUDIO8585   THE POSTER CLUB   2021

Studio8585
The Poster Club

ART DIRECTION   GRAPHIC DESIGN   PHOTOGRAPHY   WEB DEVELOPMENT
MARIO DEPICOLZUANE   BENJA PAVLIN   ANA ŠANTL   STRØM WORKS

ANIMATION   DESIGN ASSISTANCE   STYLING   CHARLOTTE SKYTTE
JOVANA ĐUKIĆ   IVA PRIMORAC   PRISZCILLA VARGA   DAUGBJERG

A small start can lead to big things, and that is a sentiment that certainly rings true for Studio8585 and its redesign of The Poster Club. What began as a slight refresh for this Denmark-based curator of art prints quickly turned to a full-fledged rebrand. "Initially, nothing really felt like the right step forward," says Mario Depicolzuane. "We allowed for ample revisions, and it was through those explorations that the client concluded they would like to go even further."

Over the course of two years, Depicolzuane's studio worked closely with The Poster Club's founder Thomas Nissen on a strategic and visual identity redesign spanning every brand touchpoint, from packaging, stationery, and print collateral to social media templates, and art direction for the e-commerce platform. A once stark

and minimalist identity hence began to incorporate an artistic touch, allowing for a more expressive range and better reflecting the emporium's international sensibilities along with its Scandinavian roots.

With this in mind, a newly designed baroque-style typeface family, Epicene from Klim Type Foundry, lends this refresh a sense of universality, while a toned-down monochrome palette showcases the brand's heritage. Once these primary design elements were established, photography took center stage. After all, The Poster Club relies heavily on communication channels, especially its social media accounts, newsletters, and website—platforms with imagery that translate its values to its audience. Because The Poster Club already had a strong photographic language and a

large database of images, Depicolzuane's job was to find an appropriate way to elevate these brand assets to the next level. To do so, he and the Studio8585 team sought collaborators "who we could trust to take our direction and execute it better than we could imagine."

For the initial roll-out, they charged photographer Ana Šantl with the task of creating an "aspirational photographic universe" that could inspire artists and customers alike. "Ana was the perfect choice because of her poetic sensibility, both in terms of how she frames the shots and her final retouch of the images," says Depicolzuane. "As a graphic designer, my bias towards typography is clear. But as an art director, I believe that photography matters now more than ever."

DIGITAL—For any online business, an e-commerce platform is of the utmost importance. As such, Studio8585 collaborated closely with Copenhagen-based digital transformation agency Strøm Works to develop a website for The Poster Club that allows more editorial expression, while maintaining an optimized online shopping experience for their client's customers.

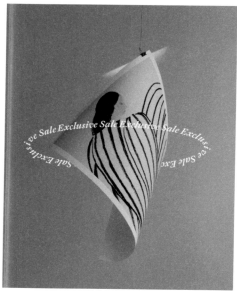

DUPLEXED AND FOILED BUSINESS
CARDS REFLECT THE TACTILITY
OF THE BRAND

JOURNAL / April 2021

In a Moment of Stillness

We met Leise Dich Abrahamsen in her atelier: A place that has been built and conceptualized for decades. Leise and her art quietly hum of experience, resulting in a juxtaposition that keeps surfacing during our conversation.

"I always end up with the same result: That my art signifies a place of calmness," Leise tells. "There is so much noise in the world. We run around aimlessly and the next crisis is always underway." She explains that her art signifies a space of stillness, but that it is not static. "I despise stagnation: I must always be moving." A condition that seems to manifest in her life, her personality as well as in her art.

2   Details of art prints
       by Leise Dich Abrahamsen

1   Ongoing process of creation
       Leise's atelier in Frederiksberg

*When I was young my style of painting was completely figurative. Over the years
I have peeled off layer by layer—I just kept simplifying.*

In parallel to her colourful compositions,
always something in black and white

3

STUDIO
MOUTHWASH

CLIENT
AIR COMPANY

YEAR
2022

MOUTHWASH Studio
Air Company

ART DIRECTION
MOUTHWASH STUDIO

GRAPHIC DESIGN
MOUTHWASH STUDIO

3D VISUALISATIONS
SERVICES GÉNÉRAUX
DEAN GIFFIN

BRANDING DESIGN
MONIKER

WEB DEVELOPMENT
RAFA COBIELLA

The climate crisis is no small matter, so when Air Company approached Mouthwash, its team jumped at the opportunity to focus on a different narrative, one with a more optimistic outlook. After all, it isn't every day that designers are posed with such a serious question as, "What if Earth's greatest threat could also be its greatest ally?"

Tasked with supporting the New York-based engineering company's transition from theoretical possibilities to present-day solutions, Abraham Campillo, Alex Tan, Mackenzie Freemire, and Ben Mingo began to unpack their client's mission, exploring, as they suggest, "what it looks like when we understand carbon as a protagonist in our story." As they unearthed more about Air Company, which captures and repurposes carbon dioxide, and its values, they determined that its offerings were best positioned between the luxury and

technology sectors. Working alongside the San Francisco studio Moniker, Campillo, Tan, Freemire, and Mingo evolved the brand with a new logo, wordmark, and a refined, mostly monochrome, palette. These elements live across digital spaces, printed matter, staff uniforms, perfume bottles, and even jet engines. "They reveal to a global audience what the future of sustainable innovation looks like," say the partners.

With these basic branding components in place, Mouthwash set out to inject Air Company with some fashionable flair. To launch Air Eau de Parfum, the first fragrance made almost entirely from air, and Airmade, the first jet fuel made entirely from captured CO_2, they produced visuals in collaboration with the Paris-based creative bureau Services Généraux. To tie together industry-spanning products like these, Campillo, Tan, Freemire, and Mingo centered their

campaigns around an immersive and impactful storytelling experience. Treating "everything like a high-end piece of jewelry, magnifying it both literally and figuratively," they elicit an expression that is at once stark and powerful.

In turn, Mouthwash translated this approach to the Air Company website, aiming to leave visitors with a clear understanding of who Air Company is, what exactly they are working on, and how it applies to day-to-day life. Its purpose is to communicate and visualize, or as the studio imagines it, "to connect the left and right sides of the brain." While the digital platform is their pièce de résistance, the Mouthwash founders maintain that a consistent visual identity and messaging strategy—whether on an invoice template, billboard, or landing page—are the keys to Air Company's potentially transformative success.

DESIGN—While Air Company is a forward-thinking venture, Mouthwash shied away from the growing trend for brands like these to feel futuristic in design. The Air Company symbol—an abstract take on the letter "A" that forms an upward-pointing arrow—is a "beacon of sustainable innovation."

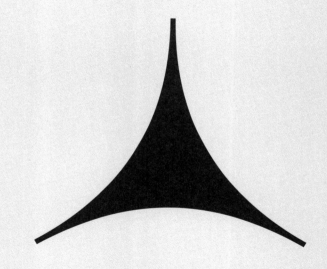

AIR COMPANY

THE SKYWARD-FACING LOGO
FOR AIR COMPANY BALANCES ITS
STRAIGHTFORWARD WORDMARK

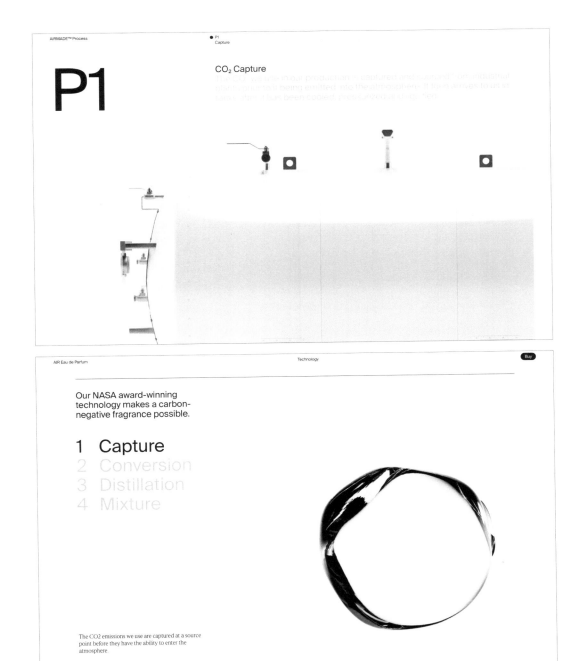

AIRMADE™ Process

● P1
Capture

P1

CO₂ Capture

Our NASA award-winning technology makes a carbon-negative fragrance possible.

1 Capture
2 Conversion
3 Distillation
4 Mixture

The CO2 emissions we use are captured at a source point before they have the ability to enter the atmosphere.

AIR Eau de Parfum   Technology   Buy

A flexible digital system is essential for this carbon-conversion innovator, whose potential customers and audiences range from industry experts to everyday consumers.

Creating A
Pathway
Towards Global
Decarbonization

AIR Applications

● 01   New solutions for industry-wide innovation

Climate change stands before us as the most pressing and complex
challenge our society faces. Carbon, the building block of life, is
threatening the way we live. Decades worth of inaction and
complacency now pose irreversible implications.

Luckily, our planet's most-abundant pollutant, can also be its
greatest ally. The technology we've developed through carbon
conversion and utilization will serve as the blueprint for industry-wide
decarbonization, freeing us from over a century-long dependency on
fossil fuels.

AIR COMPANY

Eau de Parfum

45MM

78MM

50ML / 1.75 fl oz

SKU

AIR 541650–19138181513	Chrome	
AIR 541650–19182121311	Black	●
AIR 541650–1912389205	White	○

80ML / 2.7 fl oz

SKU

| AIR 541680–19138181513 | Chrome | |
| AIR 541680–19182121311 | Black | ● |

AIR COMPANY

AIR COMPANY

MORGAN SPARKES

DIRECTOR /   (718) 313-3029
BUSINESS   HELLO@AIRCOMPANY.COM
DEVELOPMENT

IG   AIRCOMPANY
WWW   WWW.AIRCOMPANY.COM

AIR COMPANY

Invoice # 01234

John Baker
1035N Broadway
Los Angeles 90012

AIR Eau de Parfum $220
Chrome / 50ML

Paid $220.00
VISA   **** **** **** 1234

TYPOGRAPHY—Known for their simple typographic systems, the Mouthwash team employed Swiss Typefaces' premiere grotesk Suisse Int'l as Air Company's primary typeface, complementing the bespoke "AIR" lettering they developed for its logomark.

MINIMALIST AND MONOCHROME
DESIGN SUITE FOR AIR COMPANY

AIR COMPANY

VI

Design

Thinking with Design

Articulation & Expression

"There is no room for sloppiness, for carelessness, for procrastination," wrote the late visionary and acclaimed graphic designer Massimo Vignelli in his 2010 manual *The Vignelli Canon*. "Design without discipline is anarchy, an exercise of irresponsibility." When developing a brand identity, from its ideation to articulation, graphic design is our primary vehicle and, as such, one we must drive with great care.

Broadly defined as the conversion of ideas into a visual language, design does more than make things look pretty or provocative. Once we have established a shared vocabulary with our client, we are entrusted to transform it into sentences and fully formed stories. We are, in essence, translating a system of values, a philosophy, and even a lifestyle into an approachable and intelligible form.

Design is both a science and an art. We are guided by data, research, and equations as much as we are by our own creative intuition and imagination. We problem solve by skillfully selecting and rearranging our building blocks, basics like color, shape, line, texture, and scale. To operate as efficiently as a well-tuned engine, our knowledge of these components is therefore paramount. When we encounter obstacles, we try to overcome them by reading guides and books, listening to experts, and consulting our peers.

We then construct elements—logotypes, color palettes, and typography schemes—that represent the brand. They must be able to function individually while relating to each other and working as a whole. Colors, for example, can evoke emotions and set the tone, while layouts and underlying grid principles can provide both structure and unique expressions. People often relate a brand's identity with a symbol—Vignelli's American Airlines eagle, the bitten apple, or the swoosh—but the process involves so much more. How do these shapes and figures interact with a picture or a headline to create a website, a business card, uniforms, or packaging? Design is our primary means of integrating these distinct elements into a cohesive visual system, and an indispensable way of applying them to a wide range of assets.

"We design things which we think are semantically correct and syntactically consistent," asserts Vignelli, "but if, at the point of fruition, no one understands the result, or the meaning of all that effort, the entire work is useless." If we want people to listen, we ought to speak clearly. We must not only think of ourselves or our client, but our audience. After dedicating the necessary time and attention to discovery, we have a firm grasp on the cultural context that the brand exists within, and we tailor our design to its community's needs and preferences. We strive to elicit emotional responses and establish long-lasting relationships, and we do so by using our creative brief as a map to cultivate clarity.

Visual strength is equally paramount. An identity's tenacity may come from bold choices, illustrations, and typefaces that make a statement. Yet delicacy can also hold great power. Sometimes it is the subtle materials and textures that prove most transcendent. Dieter Rams famously remarked that "good design is unobtrusive." Though the German product master was responsible for creating calculators, coffee makers, and clocks rather than graphics, this design principle holds true. We must, as he says, "leave room for the user's self-expression."

We often lean into well-established visual archetypes, from stark and minimalist to nostalgic and decorative. We carefully consider historic, present-day, and future trends to safeguard ourselves from clichés—or worse, plagiarism. This cautious approach, much like regular maintenance, ensures that we stay on track and create a recognizable yet honest identity for our client.

There are countless routes to our destination, but we all operate within a set of rules and parameters, some tried-and-true and others self-imposed. Discipline, writes Vignelli, is the "bag of tools that allows us to design in a consistent manner from beginning to end." With it, we can develop an identity that stands apart in a sea of traffic.

Astrid Stavro

*Learning Lessons
from a Luminary of Design*

As part of the bold, typographic identity system for the Teatre Principal de Palma, Stavro and the Atlas team produced collectible printed catalogs for each of the performing arts center's opera and ballet programs.

Thanks in part to her lifelong fascination with words and images, the award-winning creative director Astrid Stavro is something of a graphic design savant. Her story begins at her father's printing press and publishing house. "I loved everything about it," Stavro recalls of her childhood playground. "The smell of the ink and paper, the sound of the presses, the crackling of the hardwood floors and high ceilings." Within those walls, she witnessed the evolution of printing techniques—lead type set by hand, linotype and monotype, offset printing, and photocomposition. Experiencing the process of bookmaking, from editing and typesetting to printing and binding, all under one roof proved a magically formative experience.

With a profound enchantment for text of all kinds, Stavro went on to study literature and philosophy, falling deeply into the worlds created by influential minds like Jorge Luis Borges, Aldous Huxley, William Faulkner, Arthur Rimbaud, and Jean-Paul Sartre. Their books have, as Stavro explains, "been my best teachers." But it is also in this very period, while diving into literature's greats, when everything shifted. A friend gifted Stavro a copy of *Interview* magazine, designed at the time by the provocative Tibor Kalman.

2

Her reaction to seeing the pages for the first time was electric. "The way," she remembers, "in which images and text playfully brought the content to life changed my entire course."

Born in Trieste, Italy, Stavro has long maintained a nomadic spirit. Growing up in Madrid and living in the likes of Boston, New York, The Hague, and London, her affinity for mobility extends to her far-reaching, prolific career. After receiving a bachelor's degree at Central Saint Martins and a master's at the Royal College of Art, Stavro opened up shop in Barcelona, rooting herself in the publishing and cultural sectors for a decade.

In 2013, she opted for something out of the city, co-founding a brand and design consultancy with Pablo Martín in Palma de Mallorca. The duo named it Atlas, a nod to the firm's global reach. Together, Stavro and Martín quickly put together an esteemed client roster featuring publishers Phaidon and Laurence King, Jaime Hayon and Jasper Morrison's fashion brand Jijibaba, and *Elephant* magazine (for the latter, they redesigned the publication and created practically new identities for each of the 11 issues during their tenure).

Stavro and Martín had already contributed to multiple branding projects for Mallorca-based Amadip Esment, a nonprofit organization that aims to improve quality of life for people with intellectual disabilities, when they took on the task of dreaming up an initiative for the company's 50th anniversary in 2012. Then based on the island, the duo had become inspired by the vernacular design of the octagonal boxes that hold *ensaimadas,* the quintessential Mallorcan pastry. But older packaging references were growing increasingly difficult to come by. This absence became their canvas for a creative overhaul.

"We invited leading designers, photographers, and artists from around the globe to design stickers for the boxes," says Stavro. Their brief for "EnsaimadArt," as it came to be known, was straightforward, with one succinct question: "Can a sticker have a positive impact on society?" Almost immediately, submissions began pouring in from Wim Crouwel, Lucienne Roberts, Javier Mariscal, Dean Poole, and dozens of others. The humble project turned worldwide phenomenon brought people together in solidarity for a noble cause. The limited-edition boxes became such a hit with visitors that the product was even launched at the Palma de Mallorca airport.

For Stavro, brands are not simply a logo or a tagline. They are an experience, and the truly great ones utilize "design with a capital D." She looks to Nike, Apple, and Google, all of which maintain identities that are simple yet memorable. "The biggest design choice they make," Stavro posits, "is to stay true to themselves, their values, and their promise." With markets and, in turn, consumer demands in a state of constant flux, tapping into emotions is of utmost importance.

When constructing an updated identity for renowned terrazzo and tile manufacturer Huguet, Stavro found connection with the company's CEO Biel Huguet over their

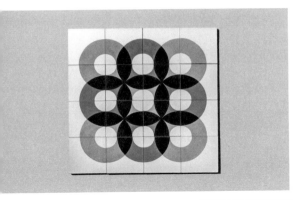

3

4

Huguet

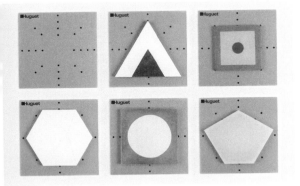

5

2 — POSTER DESIGN FOR THE MARIA CANALS
    INTERNATIONAL PIANO COMPETITION
3 — TILES DESIGNED BY MATT WILLEY FOR HUGUET
    AND PENTAGRAM PROJECT CURATED BY STAVRO
4 — TILE DETAILS FOR HUGUET
5 — HUGUET WORDMARK AND PACKAGING

shared appreciation for experimental approaches and their belief in design as a tool for transformation. The family-run business had been manually crafting beautiful, tailor-made pieces since 1933 and, with the help of Stavro and Atlas, gained a total refresh and inventive packaging solutions. She summarizes her process into the "Four Ds": define, develop, design, and deploy. "Every design decision has to be firmly rooted in this strategy," she emphasizes, "which lends to cohesiveness and effectiveness." Each project comes with its own set of challenges, and according to Stavro, close collaboration like this one is always the answer. With an ability to be selective, picking partnerships comes down to two simple things—courage and trust.

Five years on from the inception of Atlas, Stavro was invited to join Pentagram as a partner, a prestigious post she held for three years. Building on her established relationship with Huguet, Stavro brought together fellow Pentagram partners to develop a new project, culminating in a bespoke assemblage of tiles and other unique objects. With creative colleagues including Yuri Suzuki, Sascha Lobe, and Jody Hudson-Powell, a design approach blending material craft with digital technique gave way to a collection made entirely with local and sustainable materials. Stavro again emphasizes that innovative projects like these are a direct result of personal and professional relationships nurtured over years.

Most recently, owing to her extensive portfolio and network, Stavro was tapped by Collins to become its vice president and creative director, the latest feather in her cap. Today, she likens identity development to the harmonious mix of sounds in a symphony, where tone of voice, color, typography, composition, and photography are the instruments. "Just as a beautiful piece of music can evoke powerful emotions," Stavro explains, "the skillful orchestration of these visual elements can create captivating and memorable visual languages." With an illustrious array of experiences under her belt, she has amassed a design bible of her own. "A memorable brand," Stavro says, "is always built on a combination of consistency, uniqueness, simplicity, emotional appeal, storytelling, relevance, value, and authenticity."

Stavro admits that it can be challenging to stay up-to-date in our modern, hyper-connected world. But she has plenty of advice to share when it comes to staying grounded. "Never work for money," she proclaims. "Be a problem seeker, not a problem solver. The most difficult things are often the most rewarding." The list goes on. Approach every project with energy, passion, commitment, and conviction. See clients as allies, and not enemies. And above all, be curious. "I find inspiration in pretty much everything," she muses, "from the wonders of nature to Ludwig Wittgenstein's passion for making kites. The wider we cast our nets, the richer our work will be."

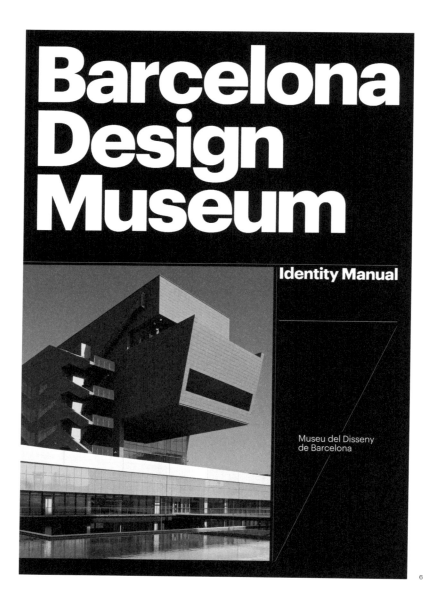

The double identity for the Barcelona Design Museum and Design Hub Barcelona, the building that houses it, is inspired by their unique location. A simple connecting line based on the city square at the junction of three of the most important thoroughfares manifests itself graphically across applications.

6 — PRINTED MATERIAL FOR THE BARCELONA DESIGN MUSEUM
7 — SPREADS FROM THE BARCELONA DESIGN MUSEUM'S IDENTITY MANUAL
8 — TYPOGRAPHIC IDENTITY FOR MAKER MILE

Bielke&Yang

Christian Bielke and Martin Yang may have met in design school, but their bonds weren't forged over a shared love of type and grids. Rather, the two, both DJs, connected over music. After graduating, they went on to earn their stripes at other design studios before embarking on an adventure of their own, one based on a clear mission: to collaborate with people who do good in the world—and to say no to anything less. As such, when establishing their studio Bielke&Yang, choosing the right person for each job has been a priority for the founders, always superseding growth for growth's sake. Today, with a carefully amassed crew of 20, they take great pride in being one of Oslo's few remaining independent firms. After just over a decade in business, they're still marching to the beat of their own drum.

1

2

What phase of brand identity development, if any, goes most overlooked? Discovery. No matter what form our design takes, we always begin by investing a lot of time understanding our clients, the business, their target audience, and the specifics of the project at hand. With patience, we have refined our process to include in-depth research and interviews before diving into the development of an identity itself.

Building trust is critical, giving us more space to craft solutions that are in tune with the client's needs while allowing us to push the boundaries of a particular industry or niche. We develop a relationship based on close collaboration through small, iterative steps and frequent meetings, ensuring effective communication and alignment. In-depth discovery makes the rest of the process fun and enjoyable because both sides are invested in the outcome. We're firm believers that our dedication to this phase is what makes collaborating with us—or independent studios like us—so special.

How do you create stand-out work in a landscape rich with intriguing visual identities? We constantly strive to deliver that elusive "X factor" that sets a project apart and makes it truly unique. We are driven by a desire to go beyond the ordinary. For us, strategy and creativity are inseparable companions that work side by side to produce exceptional results. Simultaneously, we can't put our own self-expression on a pedestal—what truly benefits the client is priority. We wholeheartedly believe that serving our client's best interests and crafting solutions that align with their goals and aspirations leads to work that resonates and achieves the most meaningful results. While developing aesthetically pleasing designs may seem effortless, ensuring their long-term effectiveness is the true challenge. Good design is sustainable design. We want our work, be it a signage system or an online store, to last.

How, then, do you achieve that longevity with your design solutions? The advent of the internet and social media has accelerated the dissemination of trends, allowing designers to discover and adapt to new styles and ideas more quickly than ever. However, while trends can offer inspiration, there is the potential danger of falling into a cycle where designs become derivative and lack originality. We strive to avoid this type of over-reliance and instead focus on more conceptual ideas to create designs that transcend passing fads. Striking the right balance requires a deep understanding of the design

1 — WORDMARK FOR OSLO'S CAFÉ PLATZ
2 — INTERIOR PHOTOGRAPHY FOR CAFÉ PLATZ

3

4

5

3 — CUSTOM TYPEFACE FOR THE ADRIAN BRINKERHOFF
     POETRY FOUNDATION
4 — BARNEOMBUDET'S BESPOKE WORDMARK IN
     COLLABORATION WITH TYPE DESIGNER BOBBY TANNAM
5 — LOGO AND ILLUSTRATION FOR BARNEOMBUDET
6 — PACKAGING AND TYPOGRAPHY FOR KALIT

landscape, thoughtful consideration of client objectives, and an ability to foresee potential saturation points in the market. By taking a more theoretical approach, we can infuse our work with a sense of purpose and meaning, producing solutions that our clients and their audiences can connect to on a deeper level.

Ultimately, the goal is to create identities that are conceptually robust and can tolerate being refreshed. The key lies in thoughtful and intentional design choices, incorporating unique elements and establishing a strong bedrock of enduring design principles.

In your experience, what type of business is the most difficult to work with? It's no secret that the public sector is the most challenging market to navigate from a design and brand perspective. In 2018, we worked with Barneombudet, Norway's official advocate for children and young adults, to help them establish a new position, visual identity, and tone of voice.

We sought to intimately understand Barneombudet's mission and values, forming a solid foundation for the subsequent design process. We devised an approach that would involve all of the different decision-makers—the advisors, project workers, lawyers, administrators, and communication strategists. Recognizing that many of these stakeholders were unfamiliar with design processes, we devoted significant time to educating them on the various stages and their importance. We conducted workshops, one-on-one interviews, and exercises to guarantee that all opinions and perspectives were considered.

Building trust proved essential yet again. Developing an environment where everyone feels respected and heard—encouraging open dialogue, active listening, and constructive feedback—allowed us to traverse what might have been a more difficult project with ease.

Do other clients tend to come in with any awareness of design processes? Business owners have certainly become more knowledgeable in the realm of design and branding, demonstrating a better understanding of what they seek from the outset. We have witnessed a shift in our ability to convey that a logo alone cannot solve every branding challenge. Today, we are able to emphasize the significance of holistic branding—communication, strategy, tone, content, and visual personality—with less pushback.

What does a shift in design literacy mean for a studio like yours? We love learning new things and pushing our clients to do the same. We are constantly maturing and expanding our knowledge as a studio, which directly influences our approach. In many ways, we aim to embody the sponge, eagerly absorbing new insights and information to enhance our capabilities and deliver exceptional results.

Serotonial
Eau de parfum
1.7 FL.OZ (50ML)
kalit
Corniche
Eau de parfum
1.7 FL.OZ (50ML)
kalit
Medina
Eau de parfum
1.7 FL.OZ (50ML)
kalit
Serotonial
Eau de parfum
1.7 FL.OZ (50ML)
kalit

7

Bielke&Yang linked The Conservatory with its founder's other project Maaemo by employing the custom typeface it developed with Colophon Foundry in 2017 for the three-Michelin-star restaurant.

Norwegian Presence hosts an annual exhibition during Milan's Design Week, and each time, Bielke&Yang devise an entirely new identity—from color palette to photography direction—based on the year's theme and content.

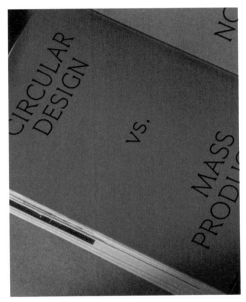

8   9

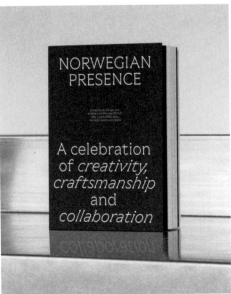

10

As a direct effect of this thinking, we started our sister company Bow in 2022. Specializing in photography, film, and copywriting, the atelier—our content partner and a natural extension of Bielke&Yang—has already collaborated independently with many brands in Norway and with other design studios.

Our in-house method to working with visual identities has also transformed significantly since we started the studio. Rather than treating a brand as a static entity, we now recognize the need for flexibility in order to keep up with the dynamic nature of modern systems. In our first development phase, we pinpoint different components of the brand that require varying degrees of adaptability. Some elements, such as the logo, wordmark, colors, and typography, should form a core base and remain relatively consistent, providing stability and recognizability. Other elements, like illustration styles, animation, or photographic styles, can be more malleable and evolve over time. As designers, we need to think of a brand as a living organism that develops and adjusts in perpetuity.

8 — BADGE DESIGN FOR 2022 NORWEGIAN PRESENCE
9 — INTERIOR SPREAD IN THE 2021 NORWEGIAN PRESENCE EXHIBITION BOOK
10 — 2023 NORWEGIAN PRESENCE EXHIBITION BOOK COVER

STUDIO   CLIENT   YEAR
1/1 STUDIO   FRAN MILLER   2018

1/1 Studio
F. Miller Skincare

CREATIVE DIRECTION   GRAPHIC DESIGN   PHOTOGRAPHY   MICHAEL KAZIMIERCZUK
NATASHA SAWICKI MEAD   NATASHA SAWICKI MEAD   BRENT GOLDSMITH   CHARLIE SCHUCK
                            NATALIE THOMPSON   JUSTIN ARANHA

Four years after developing her signature face oil—a response to the lack of natural skincare products available on the market—Fran Miller found herself with a comprehensive collection of botanically based products under the eponymous label F. Miller. She then needed a new brand identity, something that could better reflect and communicate her deep-seated values. And so she approached 1/1 Studio.

"Eschewing hyperbolic marketing language, Miller names her products simply after their primary use: Face Oil, Hair Oil, and Eye Oil," explains Natasha Sawicki Mead. "We took our cues from that approach," she continues, "and explored how they could be translated into a similarly pared-back design language, focusing only on the essentials." The result is an identity centered around typographic clarity, uniform design, and an elegant yet practical packaging suite. "Working with independent brands means coming up with solutions that are feasible for production," Mead says. "Business needs, strategy, and design have to converge to achieve something distinct that supports not only the range but also the brand language."

Mead and her team chose rectangular glass bottles that provide consistent product forms across the collection. Their visually modular appeal reflects a core element of the F. Miller line: all of the offerings can be seamlessly layered and combined. Mead suggests that these architectural glass shapes also make for elegant objects, creating a play of light and shadow both in the home and in brand photography. The rectangular motif is repeated on the heavy, uncoated paper boxes, too, creating a clear line between product and package. Moreover, the interplay between these two components means that it's as enjoyable to bring a purchase home as it is to see it on the shelf. Versatility was also on Mead's mind when it came to color. The milky green Pantone that comprises the brand's primary hue proves at once unique and enduring, and works well alongside the shades of the natural oils. It is paired with a dark khaki, which affords clear legibility for the text in print and online. "Each design element," concludes Mead, "must be carefully balanced against the others."

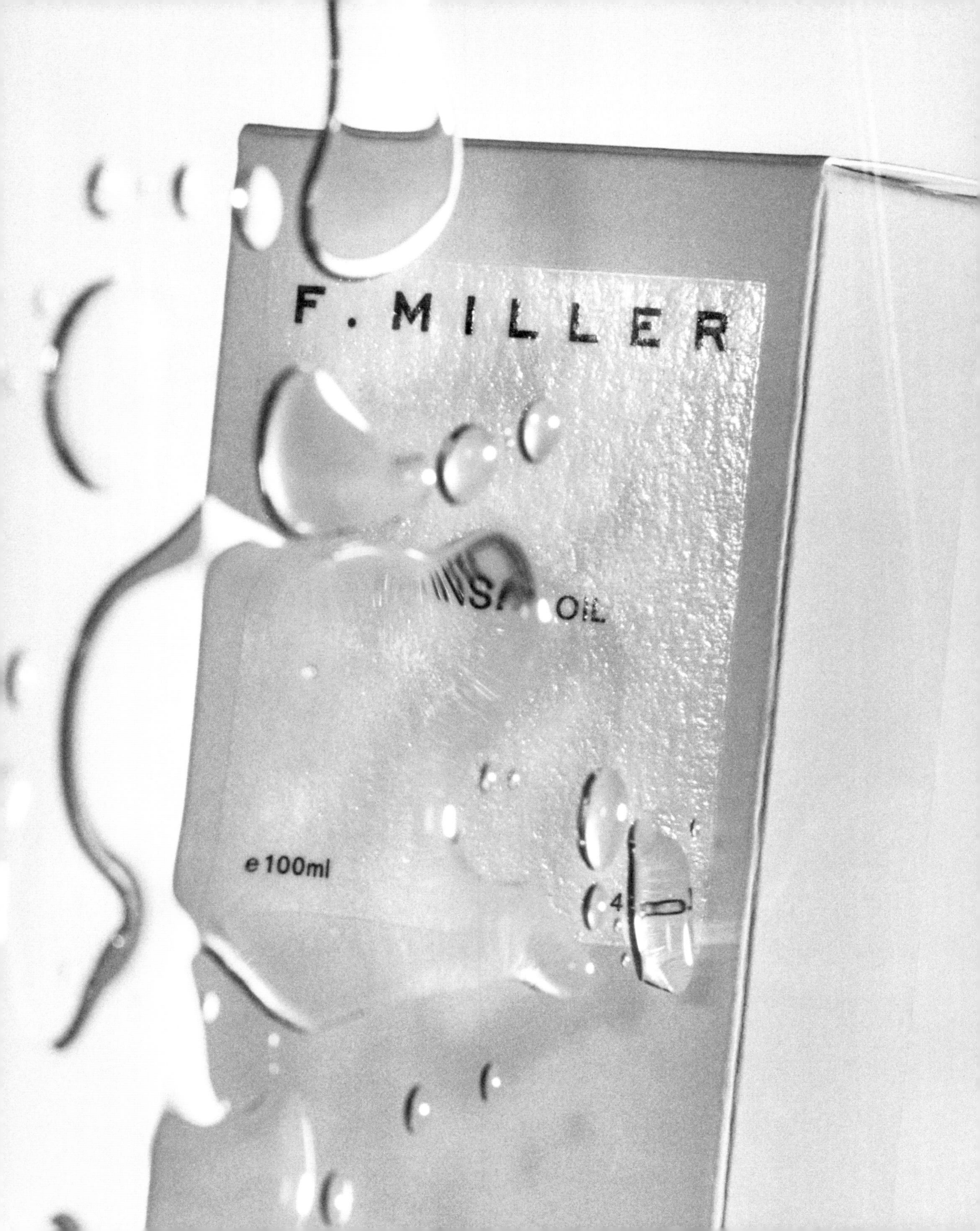
F.MILLER
OIL
e100ml

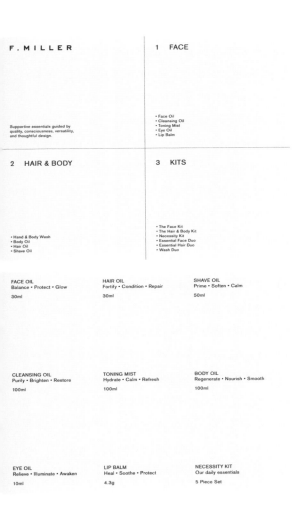

F . MILLER

Supportive essentials guided by
quality, consciousness, versatility,
and thoughtful design.

1 FACE

• Face Oil
• Cleansing Oil
• Toning Mist
• Eye Oil
• Lip Balm

2 HAIR & BODY

• Hand & Body Wash
• Body Oil
• Hair Oil
• Shave Oil

3 KITS

• The Face Kit
• The Hair & Body Kit
• Necessity Kit
• Essential Face Duo
• Essential Hair Duo
• Wash Duo

FACE OIL
Balance • Protect • Glow

30ml

HAIR OIL
Fortify • Condition • Repair

30ml

SHAVE OIL
Prime • Soften • Calm

50ml

CLEANSING OIL
Purify • Brighten • Restore

100ml

TONING MIST
Hydrate • Calm • Refresh

100ml

BODY OIL
Regenerate • Nourish • Smooth

100ml

EYE OIL
Relieve • Illuminate • Awaken

10ml

LIP BALM
Heal • Soothe • Protect

4.3g

NECESSITY KIT
Our daily essentials

5 Piece Set

F . MILLER

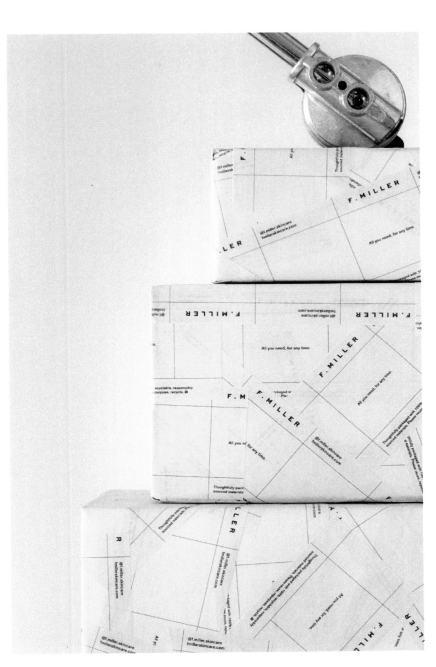

DESIGN—By organizing the visual system around the classic
design principles of a line-based grid, Mead ensures that the
F. Miller brand remains grounded in its values. "The tone, then,
comes from layering in imagery, color, and texture," she says.

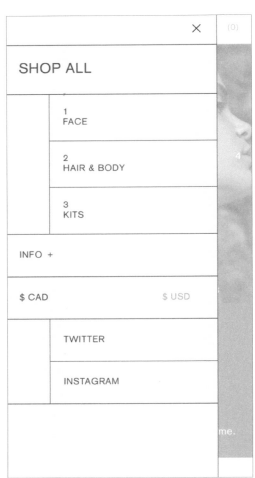

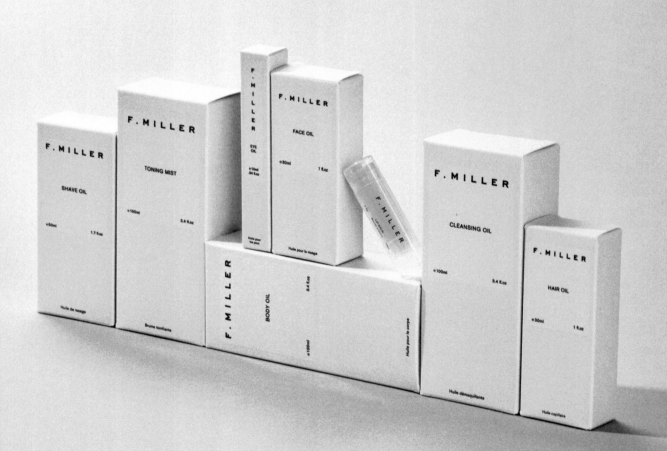

TYPOGRAPHY—1/1 Studio selected Berthold's Akzidenz-Grotesk as the primary brand font for its neutral appeal and elegant low x-height. The idiosyncrasies of this digitized historic typeface, often associated with the International Style design movement, differentiates it from modern counterparts. "These quirks add a human touch," reflects Mead, "which is important in balancing the overall tone, edited but not cold."

STUDIO   CLIENT   YEAR
TRIC   HECTOR'S DELI   2017

TRiC
Hector's Deli

CREATIVE DIRECTION   PHOTOGRAPHY   PACKAGING PHOTOGRAPHY
TRISTAN CEDDIA   JOSH ROBENSTONE   JANA LANGHORST
RICK MILOVANOVIC   ANNIKA KAFCALOUDIS

PACKAGING DESIGN   INTERIOR DESIGN   MENU & SIGNAGE DESIGN
CONTAIN DESIGN STUDIO HECKER GUTHRIE   ANCHOR SIGNS

The best designs are often born from the most unlikely of places. In 1976, Milton Glaser drew the now popular "I Love New York" logo on an envelope in the back of a taxi. Decades later, Tristan Ceddia from Melbourne design studio TRiC picked up his daughter's Etch A Sketch and dreamed up the logo for Hector's Deli, located not far from his atelier's office. While it may seem like a far cry to put Ceddia's form in the same conversation as Glaser's ubiquitous and infinitely imitated design, Hector's has become nationally recognizable thanks in no small part to this collaboration.

The logo, which harkens back to Ceddia's days both designing neon signs and producing graffiti, emerged from a sense of free and loose expression. It was honed on his daughter's classic drawing toy before being transformed into a vector, left virtually unchanged. The brand's simple mark is dotted on the sandwich paper, as well as storefront signage and a lineup of merch, perfectly matching the intended direction for the deli's identity.

From the concept itself ("the idea of a milk bar or corner store is a real fixture in Australian suburban vernacular," says Ceddia), to the branding, Hector's pays homage to the past while looking to the future. When presenting the initial direction, TRiC utilized design language from "It's Time," the slogan for the Australian Labor Party's successful 1972 election campaign led by Gough Whitlam, subsequently prime minister. Harnessing the campaign's energy, TRiC created a heavy serif wordmark, paired with contrasting bright-red Gill Sans type, thus emphasizing the brand's desire to highlight historical references alongside contemporary elements.

Working with a range of talented photographers and other collaborators, TRiC continues to shepherd Hector's art direction, helping cement the brand's reputation with striking visuals that leave a mark on customers and followers alike. A series of well-executed campaigns have rocketed the deli into a state of enduring relevance, allowing the company to expand to two new locations in 2021 and 2022. Impactful design has taken the idea of a small shop selling coffee and sandwiches "so big they burst out of your hand," and grown it into a local cultural icon.

HECTOR'S

Hector's Deli.

ALTERNATIVE WORDMARKS
FOR HECTOR'S DELI

Other merchandise, like a custom canvas tote featuring two wine pockets and an oversize Hector's tag, resonate with followers who covet the brand's visual approach.

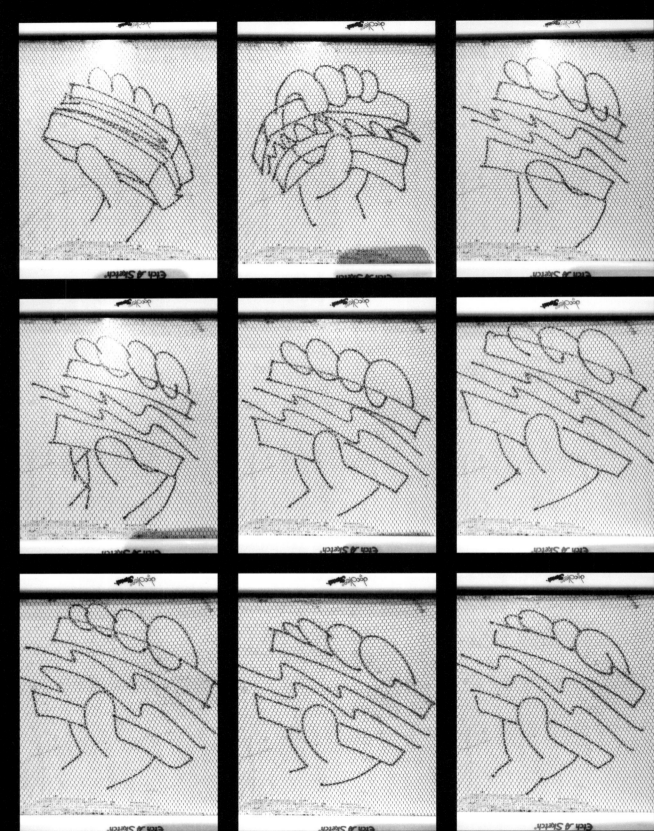

ILLUSTRATION—The logo, based on Ceddia's Etch A Sketch
doodles, resonated so well that Hector's Deli co-founder Dom Wilton
asked the team to create a similar design for their coffee program.
A simple flip of the hand and a swap of the sandwich for a cup of
coffee worked wonders, and now the second logo adorns the inside
of mugs, take-out cups, and bags of beans.

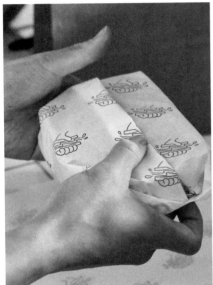

ITERATIONS OF TRISTAN CEDDIA'S
ETCH A SKETCH LOGO DESIGN

VII

Digital

Virtual Reality

Developing Digital Worlds

Eric Schmidt is what some might consider a technological pioneer. Yet, the former CEO of Google and executive chairman of its parent company Alphabet opens his 2013 book *The New Digital Age* with a stark assessment. "The Internet," he writes, "is among few things humans have built that they don't truly understand." With this in mind—and as custodians of brand identities—we must harness what Schmidt refers to as an "omnipresent and endlessly multifaceted outlet for human energy and expression." In other words, we must make the online world a valuable resource by engaging with it both critically and creatively.

Those working at the forefront of corporate visual identity design in the last century would be stunned by the gamut of branding applications on the typical designer's desk today. Tasks that might seem ubiquitous—developing websites, social media graphics, and digital banners—were a rarity less than two decades ago. In an era where terms like "data smog" exist to reference our cognitive overload, approaching the digital sphere can be overwhelming. We can look at this challenge, however, as one of our greatest opportunities to connect brands to their customers with immediacy and impact.

"On one side is the reality that audiences are more skeptical and resistant than at any time in history," confirms the American entrepreneur Jonah Sachs in his 2012 book *Winning the Story Wars*. "On the other is the fact that these same audiences, when inspired, are willing and able to spread their favorite message, creating a massive viral effect for those who win their love." We are entrusted to quickly displace uncertainty by creating functional and dynamic solutions accessible across various screen sizes and resolutions. As with environmental, editorial, or packaging design, we look to the principles of composition—scale, rhythm, contrast, proportion, and balance—to win the attention of overstimulated consumers.

In a 24-hour, two-way conversation, brands forge intimate ties with their followers, employing photography, animation, and moving images, in the feed-distributed, always-on social media universe. But in most cases, they still require a more traditional home: the humble but ever-so-advanced website. Here, we establish intuitive flows, clear messaging, and visually appealing layouts. In a 2004 blog, Jakob Nielsen, who the *New York Times* dubbed a master of website usability, explains that "with so little time to convince prospects that you're worthy of their business, you shouldn't waste even a second making them struggle with a deviant user interface."

The terrain is vast. We make deliberate decisions, grounded in a brand's priorities, about where our emphasis lies. For online brands, we focus on e-commerce design, including the less-sexy—but crucial—checkout process. Mobile apps are another environment with rules of their own, and they can be at the core of a brand's business model. Regardless of the output, we employ interactive elements to create engaging digital experiences. We bring a brand's story to life and create memorable encounters for visitors. We consider hyperlinks, scrolling mechanisms, and hierarchies. We might even devise a specific digital component, like Tinder's "swipe right" feature or Facebook's "like" button, that becomes almost as recognizable as the brand's logo.

As skilled designers, we are well versed in these online landscapes. Yet, as with any part of the process, the successful results are often collaborative. We work alongside user interface (UI) and user experience (UX) designers, brand strategists and researchers, copywriters, animators, and developers. First and foremost, we work with our audiences. With the opportunity to measure an ever-increasing array of benchmarks, we use data, wisdom, and intuition to bring an inspirational, humanist approach to our digital collateral.

Given the rate of technological advancement today, we're likely to be exploring, learning, and cultivating our digital literacy throughout our careers. It's daunting—yes. But Schmidt reminds us that, despite the great unknown, "Never before in history have so many people, from so many places, had so much power at their fingertips." As designers, we use that very power to foster the most meaningful of relationships.

Zhenya Rynzhuk

Deciphering the Secrets
of a Digital Doyenne

The website for ALET, a Copenhagen-based creative studio, hinges on unconventional design choices such as an interactive background that changes color as the user interacts with the page, and a mix of random, linear grid options.

With a portfolio of boundary-pushing digital solutions for brands ranging from the investment giant GV to the online Covid Art Museum and the bespoke diamond jeweler ORE, Zhenya Rynzhuk is making a name for herself in the industry. Born in Ukraine and now moving from location to location across the globe, Rynzhuk has always taken an unconventional approach. Before founding Synchronized Studio in 2016, she set out to design buildings, having studied architecture in Kharkiv. Her circuitous entry to the industry has nevertheless proven to be an asset in her practice. "It's no secret that the digital space is quite similar to the architectural domain," explains Rynzhuk. "We use our composition and layout skills to construct different user mechanics, flows, and journeys just like architects plan spaces to serve various functions and provide comfort for those who use them."

After working for other studios to gain design and direction experience, Rynzhuk decided to take the plunge and set up her own. In the early days of Synchronized, the group's skills revolved solely around design, but with time they entered a new phase, expanding their development capabilities to offer turnkey solutions to their clients.

2

Synchronized Studio introduces
visitors to the aviation company
Xwing with digital experiences that
include an animated grid gallery and
an interactive map.

Now working at the intersection of design and technology,
they strive to stimulate fresh and exciting ideas, always
approaching their work from new angles.

When Xwing, an autonomous aviation company
revolutionizing air travel with their breakthrough
"superpilot" technology, approached Rynzhuk, the startup
had little more than a strong logo and simple brand book.
"It felt rather flat," she recalls, "when they wanted an
elevated experience to showcase that their project was as
limitless as the sky." The firm decided to use gradients
and 3D graphics as components of the reinvented identity,
ultimately stretching the bounds of, and extending, their
overall appearance in the digital space. "Being a new
company in a traditional industry is rather challenging,"
acknowledges Rynzhuk, "so we had to make a statement
with a distinctive look that could combine trustworthiness
and a modern, forward-thinking energy."

For Synchronized, being on the cutting edge is less
of a choice and more an integral part of their DNA. "We
spend an incredible amount of time in the ideation phase,
exploring the latest technologies," affirms Rynzhuk. "We
do industry check-ups and analyze our client's competitors
to devise a different experience with the most advanced
execution." Though existing at the vanguard of digital
assets, there are certain drawbacks to creating worlds that
live almost exclusively on screens. "Physical experiences
can take advantage of the ability to engage all of the
senses," says Rynzhuk. "There are so many possibilities to
stand out, such as the look and feel—and even smell—of
a shop." Rynzhuk believes that being unique in the digital
landscape is far more difficult, particularly for niche
brands going up against mass-market players. However,
the sensual limitations of digital experiences, which engage
only our eyes and ears, are, as the designer asserts, soon to
be forgotten. "The latest breakthroughs in the field of
neurotechnology and corresponding legislation will alter the
flat web as we know it," she elaborates. "The future is very
intriguing and we must all be brave enough to embrace it."

Being on the forefront is integral for Rynzhuk, but
so is striking the right balance between the current rage
and the tried and true. "Emerging aesthetics are great
for the promotion of a new campaign," she says, "but to
ultimately build a web solution that can remain unchanged
for multiple years, we seek a more timeless foundation."
When constructing the online home for custom jewelry
maker ORE, Synchronized started with only the brand's
logo and an awareness of their target demographics and
collaborators. Existing renders and product imagery
felt underdeveloped, so Synchronized got to work on
reimagining the brand's visual language. Anchored by the
aesthetics of the classical-leaning jewelry industry while
seeking a contemporary bent, Synchronized paired an
earthy, subdued color palette with striking imagery and

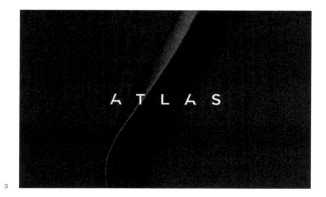

3

A SELECT GROUP OF 25 CLIENTS

4

5

motion graphics. Key to the platform are sliders that move forwards and backwards thanks to an optimized PNG sequence, and a bold, sans typeface. "There is a never-ending battle between trend and tradition," asserts Rynzhuk, "but we should accept the fact that trends push the industry forward so that new discoveries can be made, while traditions prevent brands from losing their essence and help to maintain authenticity." Or, to put it more simply, "pick your fighter."

When such a multitude of overlapping assets contribute to a brand's holistic identity, working effectively with collaborators proves essential. Having some basic understanding of adjacent fields can be beneficial, but for Rynzhuk, it all boils down to open-mindedness and communication. When GV, who recently changed their name from Google Ventures after parting ways with their former search engine parent company, sought a full visual revamp, Synchronized earned a seat at the table next to Moniker Studio. While Moniker took charge of the rebrand, Synchronized tackled the digital assets, focusing on web design and development. "It was a digitally oriented project, so we kicked off by concepting the website as soon as the overall strategy was finalized," recalls Rynzhuk. Working side by side with the Moniker team, Synchronized leveraged their close collaboration via an unhindered flow of ideas to guarantee an expedient application on the new site. "We took a similar approach with our motion ideas," says Rynzhuk. "We were able to run tests in the early stages to deliver fully animated concepts to the client." Finally, Synchronized implemented photography from Moniker, complementing the overall brand direction and cementing the end result of a successful partnership.

With seemingly endless tasks and responsibilities to juggle, Rynzhuk's role seems overwhelming. Ensuring cross-platform integration, polishing end-user experience, striving for uniqueness at every turn, and keeping apprised of the latest technological tools are only a handful of her duties in a wildly competitive field. On top of the demands of her day job, Rynzhuk's skills have earned her a spot as a judge for two organizations that honor the best of the internet: the Awwwards and the Webby Awards. She also runs the Sochnik Design Thinking School, a platform for fellow Ukrainians to study digital and graphic design and gleams when she says that over 1,000 students have graduated from their programs thus far. Wherever she finds herself next, Rynzhuk will surely be blazing a trail ahead.

2 — XWING WEB DESIGN DETAILS
3 — TYPOGRAPHY FOR ATLAS
4 — ONLINE SPREAD FOR ATLAS
5 — ORE DIGITAL EXPERIENCE

JAEMIN LEE, HEESUN KIM, AND WOOGYUNG
GEEL ARE THE DRIVING FORCES BEHIND
SEOUL'S STUDIO FNT

Studio FNT

In the realm of Korean design, Jaemin Lee, Heesun Kim, and Woogyung Geel are pioneers. When Studio FNT was born in 2006, the industry was characterized by strong divisions between disciplines like logo creation, web development, and editorial production. And so the atelier's co-founders and their team began a quiet revolution, creating holistic work based on personal interests. Studio FNT has subsequently grown to a group of 12, steadily traversing barriers and breaking taboos in the design scene. Though the excellence of the company's portfolio speaks for itself, the agency is equally committed to preserving craft, promoting equity, advocating for animal rights, and boycotting unethical collaborators. Since the 2010s, the Korean visual landscape has exploded into a hotbed of trends. All the while, Studio FNT has remained steadfast in their ways, ready to prove to other designers that another world exists beyond the fads.

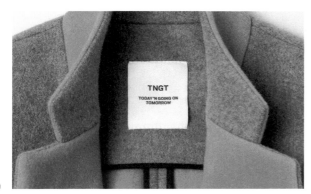

1

2

3

Can you touch on some of the overarching tenets of your studio's outlook? Seeking to align aspirations with actions, we have deliberately maintained a flexible and adaptable approach since the inception of our studio. By choosing to operate as a small organization, our expansion has been driven not by sheer scale, but by a desire to enhance our performance. It is not about having more members doing the same tasks, but rather about broadening our capabilities to encompass additional specialties such as motion graphics or 3D representation. We also prioritize client coordination. We focus on maintaining long-term relationships, as the familiarity and shared understanding cultivated over time streamlines the collaboration process. The subsequent steps become much easier.

How do you approach brands with preexisting identities? Within our organization it is a commonly shared sentiment that discarding old assets without considering their value is unwise and wasteful. Ignoring the potential of existing resources is a mistake often made by startup companies. One might argue that leveraging existing assets presents a design constraint, but it's important to acknowledge that all constraints have the potential to foster great creativity.

Even if a brand was not initially conceived with meticulous thought, there are often elements, whether they be a specific color or shape, that can be revived and given new life. Working with an existing brand offers certain advantages. The problems that need to be addressed are generally more apparent than when starting from scratch. This accessibility allows for a more focused and targeted approach in finding effective solutions. There are no inherently bad materials to work with in design—it is just a matter of how they are utilized.

As you allude to, design work always comes with certain restrictions. How do you respect those barriers while producing exciting solutions? Design, in my opinion, involves a delicate balance between control and expression. Consider a poster printed with only two colors on recycled paper: it can leave a more memorable impression compared to one printed with many colors on photographic paper. Each project comes with its unique set of constraints, such as time, budget, or the preservation of legacy assets like a logo. But as we said, those limitations often spark creative solutions.

Since 2011, we have been involved in art direction and design for the Seoul Record Fair. Instead of devising

1 — BRAND IDENTITY FOR TNGT
2 — BRANDING AND PACKAGING FOR EDIYA BEANIST
3 — PHYSICAL COLLATERAL FOR CULTURE STATION SEOUL 284

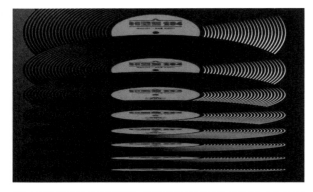

4

5

6

entirely new creative concepts for the event each year, we have followed a consistent approach where we develop designs inspired by the iconic black vinyl disk. This approach presents a unique challenge in that we must create variations while considering the future direction and maintaining a balanced aesthetic across multiple years. It might be more demanding than creating something entirely new each time, but it has allowed the Seoul Record Fair to establish a strong and recognizable identity.

Have other projects presented obstacles for your team? We took on the task of generating the identity for a broadcasting company, which included an on-air application for the broadcast screen—a domain we had not previously explored. They sought someone who could eschew cookie-cutter approaches and provide something distinctive. We were not keen on the idea of having sporadic appearances of cute, grandiose, and overstimulating 3D elements mixed haphazardly with applied typography. Instead, our method was to bring logic and reason to the design of the broadcast screen. We systematized layouts and palettes for each category and hierarchy of shows, ensuring that they could handle various types of content such as news, entertainment, culture, drama, and sports. It was more about planning and design, as opposed to mere decoration.

At first, the internal designers weren't too fond of what we came up with. They considered it flat and 2D. However, the system we devised, with its pleasing grid-like composition and range of colors, ultimately proved successful and unprecedented in Korean television. About six months later, broadcast screens imitating this flat look began to appear. We are humbled to admit that what we built is now widely recognized as a significant milestone in the realm of Korean broadcast design. In the process, our own horizons and perspectives expanded, too.

In today's digital landscape, how do you create a cohesive visual identity across various channels? The primary concern should be how sequences unfold in the digital space. Unlike offline experiences where, prompted by visual cues, consumers rely on their imaginations to fill in the gaps, online experiences require more explicit information. Moreover, online distractions can easily divert the attention of consumers from one scene to another. Therefore, it is crucial to focus on creating stimuli that can captivate attention for longer durations. We have also found success by utilizing motion graphics to explain principles and concepts more efficiently in a shorter span of time. The online space presents both constraints and opportunities. It necessitates engaging and concise content.

4 — IMAGERY FOR RECORD 284 EXHIBITION
5 — EXHIBITION BOOKLET FOR RECORD 284
6 — TURNTABLE SLIPMATS FOR THE SEOUL RECORD FAIR
7 — POSTER DESIGN FOR THE SEOUL RECORD FAIR

제7회 서울레코드페어
7TH RECORD & CD FAIR IN SEOUL
2017. 6. 17. SAT – 18. SUN 11AM – 8PM
서울혁신파크 SEOUL INNOVATION PARK
서울시 은평구 녹번동 5
무료입장 FREE ENTRANCE

주최: 서울레코드페어 조직위원회
주관: 라운드엔라운드 협동조합
후원: 서울문화재단, 서울혁신파크

www.recordfair.kr
facebook.com/recordfair
instagram: @seoul_recordfair
twitter: @round2

DESIGN—Studio FNT devised a new visual icon to represent the Korean publisher Wisdom House. The owl, which they designed by connecting punctuation marks such as commas, quotation marks, periods, and exclamation points, represents knowledge and communication.

8

9

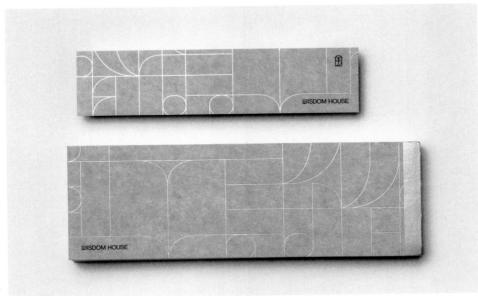

10

8 — OWL LOGO FOR PUBLISHER WISDOM HOUSE
9 — WISDOM HOUSE STATIONERY
10 — PRINT COLLATERAL FOR WISDOM HOUSE

For Studio OYK's 2022 Fall/Winter Collection "I'm Rooted, But I Flow," Studio FNT developed a quilting pattern that expresses the continual passing of time.

A strong part of your practice focuses on highlighting craft culture. How do you reconcile that emphasis with our world's vast sea of trends? While being assertive, grand, and avant-garde can be cool and admirable, we aspire to produce things that people want to own, something we ourselves would treasure on my own shelves. We remain inspired by the timeless beauty found in the distant past when things were crafted with the utmost care and dedication.

Visual trends come and go, and designers often get caught up in the latest fads. For example, in Korea, movie posters frequently featured hand-drawn or brushstroke titles. Nowadays, pointed letters, chrome textures, and 3D objects reign supreme. But have you ever experienced something that was once considered cutting-edge suddenly appear outdated? Have you ever encountered stunning designs on Instagram or a website, only to be disappointed when you saw the physical, produced, or printed version?

By adhering to our convictions and exercising sound judgment, we liberate ourselves from these passing trends. Mistakes occur when one's desire for self-expression overtakes the intended outcome of a project. It's crucial to seize opportunities and apply newly acquired skills, but it is even more important to discern what truly matters.

Culture & Education   Entertainment   News   Drama   Sports

11 — BRAND IMAGERY FOR STUDIO OYK
12 — CLOTHING TAG DESIGN FOR STUDIO OYK
13/14 — ANIMATIONS FOR BROADCASTER JTBC 2

STUDIO
MOUTHWASH

CLIENT
NEUTRA VDL HOUSE

YEAR
2022

MOUTHWASH Studio
Neutra VDL

ART DIRECTION
MOUTHWASH STUDIO

GRAPHIC DESIGN
MOUTHWASH STUDIO

PHOTOGRAPHY
ELIZABETH CARABABAS

WEB DEVELOPMENT
JASON BRADLEY

Before beginning to create a new identity for the Neutra VDL Studio and Residences, the design agency Mouthwash needed to determine which elements of the company's existing branding could be maintained and what needed updating.

"Like with owning an old home, there is a fine line between preservation and renovation," say the creative bureau's co-founders Abraham Campillo, Mackenzie Freemire, Alex Tan, and Ben Mingo. And so they turned to the Austrian-American architect Richard Neutra's decades-spanning personal archive, the 1930s facility in Los Angeles, and midcentury modernism more generally.

Rich with heritage, Campillo, Tan, Freemire, and Mingo nevertheless found Neutra VDL's existing visuality a double-edged sword. "It's easy to get lost in the references and history without thinking about the implications of the work in the present-day," the partners explain. "Is it serving our needs? Is it pushing the needle forward, or moving it in a circle?"

With this in mind, they pursued a design that retains a distinctly tactile quality. Referencing the giants of midcentury modernism, especially Bauhaus and Knoll, Mouthwash landed on a neutral color palette. The atelier infused the warm black and white tones often employed in European modernism to create a clean and industrial atmosphere with a hue of brown nodding to Neutra's aesthetics. The studio then employed Akzidenz-Grotesk, one of the first sans-serif typefaces to be widely used worldwide and a hallmark of the simplicity and accessibility found throughout Neutra's work.

Viewing themselves as digital architects rather than strictly as web designers, they addressed the online strategy for Neutra VDL as they might address the institute's physical location. Campillo, Tan, Freemire, and Mingo treated the navigation as hallways in the Neutra residence, and the pages as individual rooms. "You can peek into a room without fully going in, but you're sure to miss something in doing so," they explain. This experiential approach lends a new perspective to Neutra and his work while also fostering an inclusive, wide-reaching community. After all, Mouthwash's vision for this redesign was centered on expanding demographics and making architecture more widely available. "For the majority of us, architecture is just a means to an end—a house to live in, a restaurant to go to, an event space to attend," Campillo, Tan, Freemire, and Mingo conclude. "Taking the opportunity to shift that dynamic by opening up the history of the home to anyone with access to an internet connection was a no-brainer."

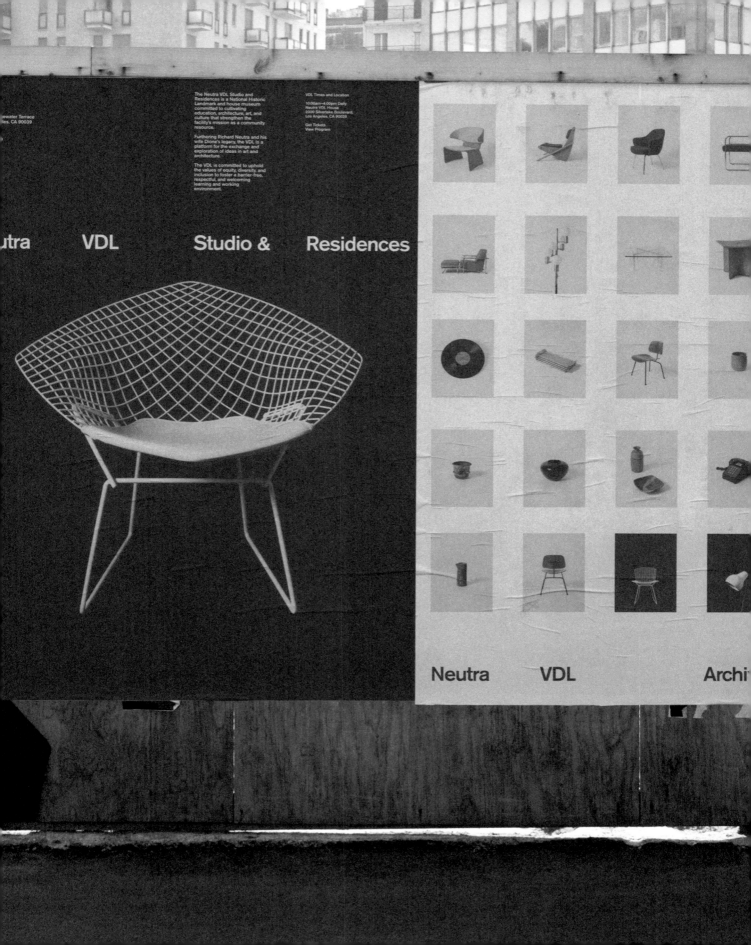

The Neutra VDL Studio and
Residences is a National Historic
Landmark and house museum
committed to cultivating
education, architecture, art, and
culture that strengthen the
facility's mission as a community
resource.

Furthering Richard Neutra and his
wife Dione's legacy, the VDL is a
platform for the exchange and
exploration of ideas in art and
architecture.

The VDL is committed to uphold
the values of equity, diversity, and
inclusion to foster a barrier-free,
respectful, and welcoming
learning and working
environment.

VDL Times and Location

10:00am–4:00pm Daily
Neutra VDL House
2300 Silverlake Boulevard,
Los Angeles, CA 90039

Get Tickets
View Program

utra   VDL   Studio &   Residences

Neutra   VDL   Archi

DISCOVERY—Campillo, Tan, Freemire, and Mingo
remind us that "as a society, we often associate rebrands
as 'out with the old, in with the new,' but that isn't a very
efficient way to reach our goals."

Neutra VDL

NEUTRA VDL'S UPDATED WORDMARK
IN AKZIDENZ GROTESK

Mouthwash focused on creating an interactive learning experience for Neutra and his legacy. Their primary question then became, "How can we make visiting the house a natural extension of that experience?"

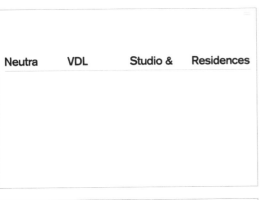

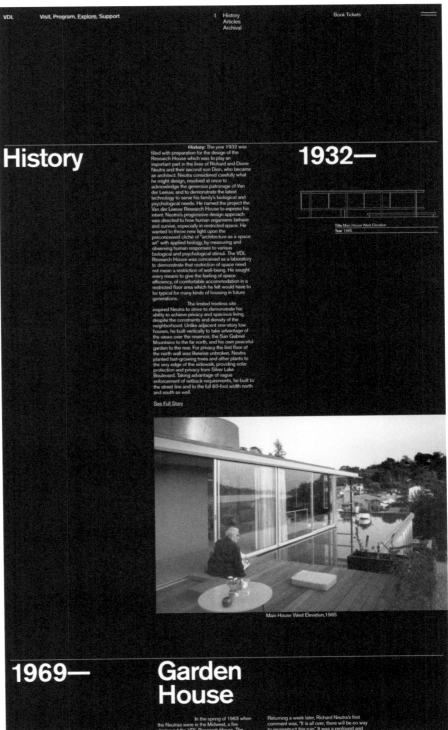

PHOTOGRAPHY—While the studio could have worked exclusively using archival imagery on the website, Campillo, Tan, Freemire, and Mingo insist that they "would have missed the mark when it comes to bringing Neutra and his work into the 21st century." In collaboration with interiors photographer Elizabeth Carababas, they instead leaned heavily on Julius Shulman's photos of Neutra's house, borrowing frames and recontextualizing the residence for its present-day purpose.

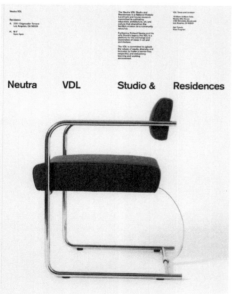

PHYSICAL—To celebrate the launch of the new visual identity, Mouthwash and the Neutra VDL Studio and Residences invited the public to a celebration featuring live music, a video installation, and a selection of limited-edition prints for sale in support of the house's preservation.

STUDIO
PENTAGRAM

CLIENT
THE MIDI ASSOCIATION

YEAR
2021

Sascha Lobe/Pentagram
MIDI

TYPOGRAPHY
GRAPHIC DESIGN
SASCHA LOBE

SOUND DESIGN
YURI SUZUKI

PHOTOGRAPHY
CINEMATOGRAPHY
KIMBERLY LLOYD

While conspiring on a revamp for the industry standard MIDI (an acronym for Musical Instrument Digital Interface), sound artist Yuri Suzuki and graphic designer Sascha Lobe bonded over music in more ways than one. During the Covid-19 pandemic, the Pentagram partners joined forces, producing a daily playlist on behalf of their renowned agency. Spanning genres from the orchestral to the electronic, featuring artists like John Cage, Arvo Pärt, Iannis Xenakis, and Cornelius Cardew, and implementing visual accompaniments, the compilations were warmly welcomed by Pentagram staff and followers working from home across the globe.

Meanwhile, Suzuki and Lobe were continuing to develop a new identity for MIDI, a nonprofit organization whose technology has pioneered and championed much of the music we enjoy today, from Kraftwerk to Nicki Minaj. The duo came to the table freshly inspired and invigorated by their ongoing collaborations. "With its cutting-edge technology, MIDI has been a game-changer for musicians, DJs, producers, educators, and artists," explains Lobe, "and so as music makers and lovers ourselves, we found a real opportunity working on this project together."

Quickly, the central question for Lobe became, "How do you create a visual identity for a brand focused squarely on sound?" The answer arrived in the form of a sonic logo and an animated M-shaped wordmark, a reference to the Stuttgart pitch, a standard for musical tuning, and the shape of Lissajous curves. The former, with a pitch beginning at 440 Hz and rising to 880 Hz, can, according to Lobe, "create a Pavlovian, or anticipatory, response." In other words: when these elements combine, they become as instantly recognizable as MIDI's product itself.

Shying away from clichés and more literal references, Lobe and Suzuki instead looked to the subtleties of soundscapes and the sentimentality of music more generally. The brand overhaul, a process that took two years, was informed by a makeover of the actual product, its most significant update in 35 years, dubbed MIDI 2.0. "We had to push beyond the 1980s-era original branding to reflect this 'future-proof' upgrade," says Lobe. For the first time ever, data can flow between instruments in two directions simultaneously. Likewise, Lobe worked with Suzuki to artfully meld their individual specialties in reciprocal fashion. "We created a mirror," Lobe says, "between sound and vision."

TYPOGRAPHY—Lobe designed a custom sans-serif typeface for an acronym that complements the M-shaped logomark with its curves, a result of experiments looking at sine waves on an oscillator. He opted to employ the 1950s type family Univers for other texts, lending the identity an air of technicality.

x–y–   x146y32   x218y95   x322y81

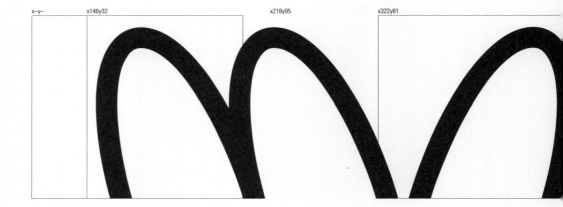

DIRECTION—In partnership with Yuri Suzuki, Lobe developed
an identity that taps into synesthesia, a complex neurological condition
that breaks down the boundaries between senses, and in this case
creates a constant interplay between the visual and the sonic.

BI-DIRECTIONAL
440 Hz

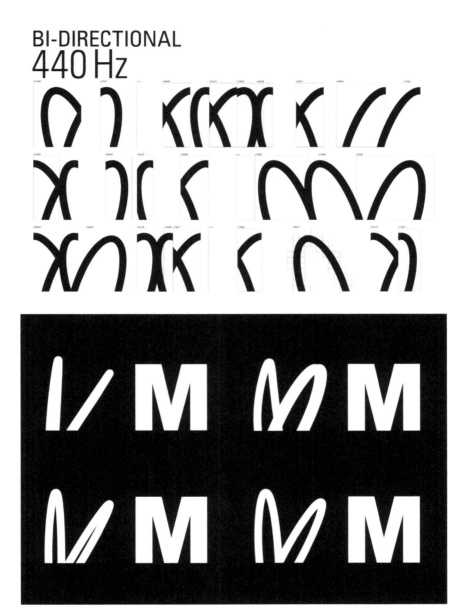

VIII

Physical

Material Matters

Creating Concrete Collateral

Presenting to a room full of designers in 1880, William Morris, the godfather of Britain's Arts and Crafts movement, laid down a golden rule. "Have nothing in your houses that you do not know to be useful, or believe to be beautiful," he declared. In a competitive, global market where simply being great is no longer good enough, his maxim has become our mantra. The brands we take on are our homes. We furnish them with all things functional and beautiful—and never extraneous—to resonate well beyond the "four walls" of the products and services they offer.

In today's digital society, branding's physical aspects, from stationery to business cards and brochures, can be overlooked. We must remember that while the digital sphere has become central to our lives, we still exist in a physical world. These two facets of brand communication need not be at odds but complementary. With so much existing on our screens, tangible assets have become more consequential than ever before. Indeed, as a result of their staying power, these resources distinguish themselves as some of a brand's most disruptive, attention-grabbing elements.

Perhaps because of the human nature of the medium, this aspect of our work can provide the utmost satisfaction. In her book *A Natural History of the Senses,* the American naturalist Diane Ackerman recalls neuroscientist Saul Schanberg explaining that touch is "far more essential than our other senses" and "10 times stronger than verbal or emotional contact." The physical has the opportunity to engage and stimulate us more fully, and we are tasked with translating that gratification to a brand's audience. We start by directing our attention towards printed collateral—flyers, postcards, invitations, packaging, or brand books. A thoughtful and well-executed combination of paper stock and print techniques can transform something like the modest logotype into a real-world story.

We build on the foundations laid in the direction phase to select materials that align with a brand's mission and values. We might opt for a touch of the unpredictable, though never solely for the sake of surprise. For a more crafted feel, we favor uncoated paper stock or special design paper with compelling embossed structures or organic finishes. To indicate a sense of precision and professionalism, we employ details like foiling. We consider sustainable materials, such as recycled paper or biodegradable plastics, that convey a brand's commitment to the environment and social responsibility.

For brands with physical spaces, we emphasize signage, providing a visual cue for consumers that creates a sense of place and belonging. Uniforms can also prove essential, particularly for service-oriented businesses like restaurants and hotels, where reinforced identity and consistency are key. But even for brands lacking brick-and-mortar outlets, experiential design has become increasingly useful. Temporary pop-up stores and events, where we explore touch as well as sound, sight, smell, and taste, allow them to create a real-life presence and personally interact with their consumers.

Because these physical components frequently require a significant budget, having print collaborators we trust is imperative to assure our clients. We choose versatile and knowledgeable printers or manufacturers that use high-quality materials and advanced techniques to guarantee results. We vet several companies, but the goal is to develop long-lasting relationships. We might even use an intermediary who helps us navigate the production process with greater ease. We go through rounds of testing and prototyping, all while considering the user experience. Packaging should be easy to manage and dispose of, signage should be clear and visible, and uniforms should be comfortable and practical.

With attention to detail, brands can create positive and memorable experiences for everyone, leading to increased loyalty and even raving fans. By combining physical assets with the digital—meaningful web, mobile, and social media interactions—we develop a brand world that is cohesive, compelling, and inclusive. If successful, we welcome visitors to the home they never knew they needed—and better yet, encourage them to stay.

Imprimerie du Marais

Exploring the World of a Storied Paris-Based Printer

In 2014, Made Thought redesigned the
identity for Imprimerie du Marais to better
reflect its firm commitment to the past,
present, and future. With a relationship that
has spanned years, the two businesses work
side by side to ensure that the printer's visual
assets evolve with the times.

We've all heard that print is supposedly dead, and while
the global demand for printed matter may have shifted
in recent years, the brain trust behind Imprimerie du
Marais never got the message. Founded in 1971 by Charles
Przedborski in the Marais neighborhood on the Rive
Droite, the Parisian atelier has been creating beautiful
materials and pushing the limits of print potential ever
since. What's more, there's no end in sight. Imprimerie du
Marais's mantra and guiding principle is, after all, *l'art du
possible.* And the reason for this is simple. Their clients and
collaborators, which include brands from Balenciaga and
Dior to the NoMad Hotel and Macallan, know that they
are the production partner who will simply never say no.

Born into a family of Polish sewage workers,
Przedborski has long lived in a world where humans and
machines are inextricable companions in daily life. Proud
of his working-class background and with deep curiosity,
fueled by a penchant for reading, he turned to printing, an
extension of his studies at the communication design and
book arts college École Estienne. The industry, he thought,
was a noble one, and with the opening of Imprimerie du
Marais, he had found a way to make his mark.

2 — MICROFOILED AND MULTILEVEL EMBOSSED DETAILS
    WITHIN THE IMPRIMERIE DU MARAIS 2019 DAY PLANNER
3 — PACKAGING FOR THE IMPRIMERIE DU MARAIS 2019
    DAY PLANNER

"Przedborski's personal environment, which formed his nerve center, was made up of typographic composition, independent journalism, abandoned local press offices, and traditional paper mills," explains Mélody Maby-Przedborski, the print master's daughter-in-law and head of development and communication at Imprimerie du Marais. Until Przedborski's son Jacky joined the company in 1995, the atelier produced stationery for Parisian ready-to-wear brands. Then, fresh out of school and inspired by the cultural momentum of the 1990s, the younger Przedborski entered into his father's well-established business with big plans. "He installed cutting-edge technology in the rue Chapon workshop," says Maby-Przedborski. "He could print litho faster, challenge the potential of foiling, and develop screen printing to produce extravagant invitations for the explosive new 'super-fashion' scene that was flourishing at the time."

For more than 30 years since, the studio has taken on some of the most challenging commissions from top fashion houses, luxury brands, and a wide range of creative institutions. While most of their peers in the industry merely provide the tools to bring a brand's vision to life in the physical world, Imprimerie du Marais takes a different approach, remaining at the vanguard of print design and production in Paris and the world at large through its London, New York, and Geneva offices.

The team provides machinery, materials, and thought-provoking ideas in equal measure. "We work closely with our clients to bring designs into reality," Maby-Przedborski elaborates. "We share our long-standing knowledge of materials, techniques, and formats, along with our established relationships with paper mills." To be sure, a commitment to explore, innovate, and make sustainable developments with their collaborators is central to Imprimerie du Marais's DNA.

Perhaps it helps that the Parisian outfit is familiar with the identity process on a more personal level, having developed a robust visual presence of its own. In 2014, it partnered with Made Thought, a leading design agency with offices in London and New York, to rebrand its business. "Working with the Made Thought team proved truly liberating," recalls Maby-Przedborski. "It helped us to understand what was truly extraordinary about our positioning and therefore, our achievements." Having learned to articulate the passion, expertise, love of craftsmanship, and sense of innovation that define it, Imprimerie du Marais has built on this experience when taking commissions from leading brands across other sectors.

With a seasoned team, the studio adapts to the exacting needs that go hand-in-hand with ambitious designs and demanding delivery dates. When the London and Seoul-based creative bureau MMBP & Associates was tasked with developing Bhutan's international brand

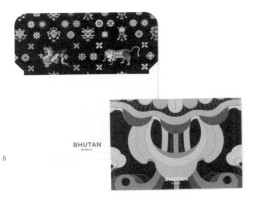

BHUTAN
believe

Bhutan's identity, rooted in the
colors of its flag and natural
landscape, extends to the likes
of cards and envelopes.

image, Imprimerie du Marais sought to capture the
nation's ambitions with equally bold print collateral. The
project required Pantone offset printing, foiling, cutting,
binding, and hand-shaping, all on recycled paper curated
by the French print-production house. "They chose
our workshops to carry out this beautiful project because
of our ability to produce such high-quality finishings at
lightning speed," says Maby-Przedborski. In the span of
a single week, Imprimerie du Marais delivered postcards,
envelopes, posters, luggage stickers, and business cards
by the thousands—all in plastic-free packaging—to Bhutan
as well as to its representatives in places like London,
Delhi, Dhaka, Geneva, and New York. Maby-Przedborski
attributes the project's success to a spirit of adventure
held by the client, design studio, and printer alike.

With that very same spirit and after 52 years in
business, Imprimerie du Marais moved its headquarters to
6 Cité Griset in Paris's 11th arrondissement. In this grand
workshop, housed within former industrial spaces and
redesigned by architects Atelier Saint-Lazare, the studio's
imagination and creativity can flourish, allowing its team
to test their clients' boundaries more than ever before.

"Printing itself has a long history, spanning at least
575 years," reflects Maby-Przedborski. "It is true, however,
that the last decade has considerably changed the way
that we perceive the printed object." In her opinion, it's a
change for the better. With a seemingly ceaseless stream
of content online, creating tangible products that are
memorable and long-lasting has become all the more
powerful. "In that respect, print really isn't in competition
with digital," Maby-Przedborski asserts. "It offers
something different and singular, something that digital
simply cannot." Printing has, it seems, returned to its
status as a premium service, with printers like Imprimerie
du Marais creating rarefied and precious objects—things
to be cherished.

Of course, it can be hard to keep up with this
constantly changing and evolving world. But the Parisian
atelier is still pushing things to the limits, while striving
to improve and learn at every opportunity. "There is
no substitute for experimentation," Maby-Przedborski
concludes. "When we bring a design to life on paper—right
before our eyes, through our very hands—that's when the
magic happens."

6

7 8

9

The Imprimerie du Marais team works closely
with Made Thought to develop a series of printed
objects from brand books to day planners that
showcase their abilities and strengths.

6 — IMPRIMERIE DU MARAIS 2023 CALENDAR
7 — CUSTOM FONT BY MADE THOUGHT FOILED ON
NOTPLA SEAWEED PAPER FOR THE 2023
IMPRIMERIE DU MARAIS CALENDAR

8 — RAISED FOILED LOGO ON THE OUTER BOX FOR THE
IMPRIMERIE DU MARAIS 2023 CALENDAR
9 — EXPERIMENTAL INNOVATIONS WITH BITMAP FOIL IN THE
IMPRIMERIE DU MARAIS BRAND BOOK *L'ART DU POSSIBLE II*

AND
ASSING
ACH
TUTION,
CREATIONS

1/1 Studio

Since childhood, Natasha Sawicki Mead has loved making things. Born at a time when the internet was only just arriving in people's homes, she began building worlds—creating digital art in Microsoft Paint and making websites to house it—on her family's newly acquired home computer. It wasn't until university, however, that she realized design, especially typography and craft through a digital medium, was what she had loved all along. After graduating, she reconnected with Joe Swann, a former classmate and an adept web developer. This reunion led to a diverse array of projects that marry their technical and design skills across platforms, spawning their Auckland-based atelier, 1/1 Studio—the only place Mead has ever worked, learning from her team, her clients, and a lengthy list of talented collaborators along the way.

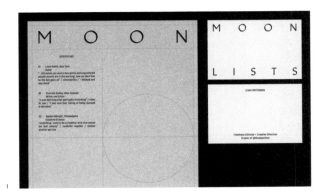

1

2

3

1 — PHYSICAL ASSETS FOR MOON LISTS
2 — STATIONERY FOR JOHNSTONE CALLAGHAN ARCHITECTS
3 — BRAND IMAGERY FOR REOME

Forming visual identities is a process. Can you walk us through your progression? Good branding honors the integrity of what it represents. It is a mirror that shows the sensory world it encapsulates, offering a nuanced reflection, adding dimensions, instilling meaning, and creating something tactile from abstract concepts. Getting to know the owner, designer, or artist behind a company is always the most important first step. We dive into their history, their values, the landscape they occupy, and how they have shifted or evolved. Understanding their ethos provides us a unique lens to work from and illuminates potential opportunities. We are always looking for those threads—ideas we can arrange and draw on to create a brand that fosters human connection.

We distill our findings through research, compiling boards that begin to evoke a certain tone. We immerse ourselves in concept development, looking at every application possible, from printed matter to packaging and digital communication. The more areas we can test, the more resolved our solutions become. When we're ready for execution, we aim to be as granular and patient as possible. The process is akin to a funnel—in the beginning, you need to stay open, slowly refining to the point of completion. Not everything will fit easily, and that's why craft is so important.

How would you define good design? We adhere to the mantra that quality work doesn't fear time. We focus on the design sensibilities that we are drawn to again and again. For me, this means design that is difficult to place in a specific moment. It is neither retro-pastiche, nor ultra-current. By its very nature, design that is created for its context is also never derivative. If we have done our job well, a brand shouldn't need to change dramatically to keep up with trends. It can evolve naturally and repeatedly over the years.

We're all surrounded by a seemingly infinite cloud of content. How do you grow visual identities that provide room for evolution in this ever-changing atmosphere? We're living in a time of incredibly high design saturation, and it can be disconcerting to see the speed at which trends proliferate. While it's great that the value of design is more widely understood than ever, there's an inherent irony that design can now feel so repetitive. The public is also increasingly wary of branding used solely as a tool to manufacture value. As such, we designers have a greater responsibility to communicate what is actually genuine. While it's important for brands to evolve their visual

INGREDIENTS/INGRÉDIENTS

(1)　Ae Gi Super Mild Soap: Sodium Rapeseedate, Water, Sodium Cocoate, Glycerin, Butyrospermum Parkii (Shea) Butter, Theobroma Cacao (Cocoa) Seed Butter, Sodium Citrate, Oryza Sativa (Rice) Powder, Oryza Sativa (Rice) Bran Extract, Hordeum Vulgare Seed Extract, Bixa Orellana Seed Oil.
(2)　Haenyeo Sea Woman Soap: Sodium Rapeseedate, Water, Sodium Cocoate, Glycerin, Mentha Piperita (Peppermint) Oil, Sodium Citrate, Magnesium Chloride (Hydrate), Potassium Chloride, Butyrospermum Parkii (Shea) Butter, Charcoal Powder, Fucus Vesiculosus Powder, Hordeum Vulgare Seed Extract.
(3)　Shaman Charcoal Soap: Sodium Rapeseedate, Water, Sodium Cocoate, Glycerin, Butyrospermum Parkii (Shea) Butter, Lavandula Angustifolia (Lavender) Oil, Sodium Citrate, Cedrus Atlantica Bark Oil, Charcoal Powder, Abies Sibirica Oil, Hordeum Vulgare Seed Extract, Santalum Album (Sandalwood) Oil.
(4)　Seshin Korean Scrub Soap: Sodium Rapeseedate, Water, Sodium Cocoate, Glycerin, Butyrospermum Parkii (Shea) Butter, Bentonite, Eucalyptus Globulus Leaf Oil, Pumice, Sodium Citrate, Sesamum Indicum (Sesame) Seed, Sea Salt, Hordeum Vulgare Seed Extract.
(5)　Boricha Tea Soap: Sodium Rapeseedate, Sodium Cocoate, Water, Glycerin, Butyrospermum Parkii (Shea) Butter, Moroccan Lava Clay, Sodium Citrate, Simmondsia Chinensis (Jojoba) Seed Oil, Bixa Orellana Seed Oil, Hordeum Vulgare Seed Extract, Jasminum Grandiflorum (Jasmine) Flower Extract.

TRAVEL SOAP SET
여행용 비누 세트

5 SOAPS & SOAP CASE

5 SAVONS ET ÉTUI À SAVON

BINU BINU

SOAP HOUSE 비누공방

5 soaps · savons × 23g ℮ 0.8 oz

PUBLIC BATH RITUALS

공중 목욕 의식

RITUELS DE BAIN PUBLIC

TRAVEL SOAP SET

SOAP & SOAP CASE · SAVON ET ÉTUI À SAVON

(EN)　Our collection of five bathhouse-inspired bar soaps, travel-sized and presented in a biodegradable, portable travel case. For discovery, gifting, or taking your favorite soaps on the go.
　Directions: For use on hands and body. Avoid contact with eyes; if contact occurs, rinse eyes with water.

(FR)　Notre collection de cinq savons en barre inspirés des bains publics, au format voyage et présentés dans un étui de voyage portable et biodégradable. Pour découvrir, offrir en cadeau ou emporter vos savons préférés pendant que vous voyagez.
　Directions: À utiliser pour les mains et le corps. Éviter le contact avec les yeux; en cas de contact, rincer les yeux à l'eau.

Manufactured For / Fabriqué Pour
Binu Binu Inc. Toronto, ON, M6R 2B2
www.binubinu.com

Made in USA / Fabriqué aux États-Unis

LOT 1213

4
5

BINU BINU
SOAP HOUSE 비누공방

6

7

4 — FOLD-FLAT PACKAGING FOR BINU BINU
5 — VESSEL DESIGN FOR BINU BINU
6 — LOGO AND TYPE DESIGN FOR BINU BINU
7 — PACKAGING AND TYPOGRAPHY FOR FLORETS

language alongside their growth, staying true to their core values yields identities that feel like beautiful and organic progressions.

To achieve that authenticity, we build partnerships with our clients based on mutual trust and respect for each other's practice—I believe that groundwork is the basis for collaboration of any kind. Design responds to problems, so we identify areas of difficulty. The best outcomes are born from a balance of understanding more concrete issues and having the creative space to explore and resolve them.

For example, our branding work for BINU BINU presented us with some unique challenges. Our client, Karen Kim, is based in Canada, so we needed English and French on the packaging suite. Because the brand is steeped in the tradition of the *jjimjilbang,* the concept of the Korean bathhouse, we also wanted to include Hangul, the native alphabet. Three languages are a lot to support on any packaging scheme, but especially on something relatively small like a bar of soap. In the end, we developed a typographic system that could create a sense of clarity and purpose across each product in the range.

Design is becoming increasingly digital in output. What role does print play in your work? Purposeful materials and techniques always prove most satisfying. Great packaging feels like a natural response to whatever is inside. I often think about how perfect greaseproof paper is for blocks of butter. I never tire of it. We used this paper, simultaneously strong and delicate, to house loaves for a local bakery in Auckland called Florets. The wrap tells the origin story of the bread, the ingredients, and their benefits. As a bonus, it also keeps the bread fresh, and you can compost it when you're done. Packaging that is fleeting and ephemeral can still be incredibly beautiful.

We also make an effort to carry concepts through on both our digital and print platforms. Working with the artist Simone Bodmer-Turner on her online store, we were inspired by vintage ceramic catalogs. We developed a horizontal side scroller that allows you to see her pieces all in a row, as if they are sitting on a shelf. When we were exploring a print insert for her orders, we translated that same idea into an accordion foldout. It looks small and compact but extends into seven panels that showcase her full collection. This was a curious case where print references influenced our digital approach, and then it came full circle with the digital site influencing our physical assets.

What resonates with you the most: print or digital? I don't see print and digital as binary. As a studio, our practice is very much focused on lending equal importance to both. We strive to find harmony between all of these elements, and in that way, the strongest print material is really the same as any other area of design—its success lies in striking

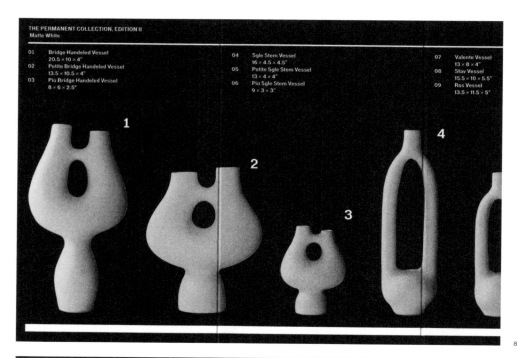

THE PERMANENT COLLECTION, EDITION II
Matte White

01   Bridge Handeled Vessel
     20.5 × 10 × 4"
02   Petite Bridge Handeled Vessel
     13.5 × 10.5 × 4"
03   Più Bridge Handeled Vessel
     8 × 6 × 2.5"

04   Sgle Stem Vessel
     16 × 4.5 × 4.5"
05   Petite Sgle Stem Vessel
     13 × 4 × 4"
06   Più Sgle Stem Vessel
     9 × 3 × 3"

07   Valente Vessel
     13 × 8 × 4"
08   Stav Vessel
     15.5 × 10 × 5.5"
09   Ros Vessel
     13.5 × 11.5 × 5"

8 — ACCORDION FOLDOUT FOR SIMONE BODMER-TURNER
9 — DIGITAL DESIGN FOR SIMONE BODMER-TURNER
10 — PACKAGING SUITE FOR LESSE

Nominated Architect
Daniel Boddam
AIA Reg No 9163

T +61 2 9660 1144
info@danielboddam.com
danielboddam.com

PO Box 1946,
Potts Point NSW 1335

@danielboddam

Mead chose Colorplan's Extract paper, which is made from recycled coffee cups, for the Guy Morgan boxes. The mustard color speaks to the hues in the company's signature face oil and balm.

that perfect balance of purpose, detail, and craft. In our digital work, we try to bring qualities that you might actually find in print—a lived-in texture, a consideration of negative space, or a typographic language that feels really specific to the site.

An exceptional visual identity offers a promise. It says, "This is worth paying attention to. This is something that has been crafted with care and intention." We keep this perspective in mind at every stage. We are meticulous about the visual tone and the details. We treat each area of the brand as important as the next, from the tactile qualities of print to the tone of the digital presence. Successful branding takes time to see in its totality. While you can measure the response of something new at launch, the biggest test is how the brand identity endures, evokes pleasure, imbues value, and, ultimately, inspires loyalty.

11   12

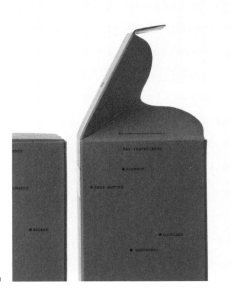

13

11 — PRINT COLLATERAL FOR DANIEL BODDAM
12 — GUY MORGAN VESSEL DESIGN
13 — PACKAGING FOR GUY MORGAN

STUDIO   CLIENT   YEAR
FNT   KOREA CRAFT & DESIGN   2020
                FOUNDATION (KCDF)

Studio FNT
Hanji

CREATIVE DIRECTION   DESIGN DIRECTION   SPACE DESIGN   VMD, DESIGN APPLICATION
HEESUN KIM   HYUNGWON CHO   LIMTAEHEE DESIGN   POINTERS

ART DIRECTION   GRAPHIC DESIGN   SOLAH KOH   UNIFORM DESIGN
JAEMIN LEE   YOUJEONG LEE   JAEMIN LEE   STUDIO OHYUKYOUNG

The production of the Korean paper *hanji* has extremely deep roots, dating back to the very origins of paper itself. When the Korean Craft & Design Foundation, an organization with a profound mission to promote native workmanship, improve quality of life, and stimulate local economies, tasked Studio FNT to both raise awareness of the formidable but dying art and remind the public of *hanji's* incredible potential, the atelier rose to the occasion, developing an entirely new Hanji brand.

Hanji is not suited to mass production and cannot be used in a printing press. Part of ancient Korean custom, it is produced from the interior bark of a mulberry tree, which is carefully removed and converted into a substance, both delicate and durable, rough and refined, and eventually transformed into the paper. The majority of

the process still relies on human hands, and the output is heavily associated with old-world ways. "Many people think of *hanji* only in terms of traditional coloring and calligraphy," say Jaemin Lee, Heesun Kim, and Woogyung Geel, "but working on this project opened our eyes to many new possibilities for the paper, which has outstanding physical properties."

Contrasting its customary uses— think the creation of watercolor tableaus portraying sweeping mountain vistas—the Studio FNT team opted to print bright geometric patterns on the paper in colors more reflective of contemporary style.

The atelier then implemented its designs on objects like fans and decorative boxes. As its founders suggest, "the intention for Hanji was to intersect the conventional with the modern in a way that feels organic."

To bring the brand to life, Studio FNT created bespoke display pieces at the 2019 Korean Craft Trend Fair. The firm also took a playful approach to distinguishing the project and defining its purpose, dreaming up a number of new stamps and seals that have traditionally adorned the margins of Korean works created with the paper for centuries. "Artists created these seals to represent ownership and convey their ideas and desires," explain the trio. At the craft fair, these stamps were then affixed to natural materials, including various types of wood and stone, in a multitude of ergonomic shapes, doubling as tactile elements that enhance the immersive exhibit.

In the end, Studio FNT didn't inspire only visitors to look at *hanji* anew. "We started exploring other uses for the paper ourselves," say Lee, Kim, and Geel, who have continued to incorporate it into other projects.

한지문화산업센터
안내서

한국어

Hanji Culture and
Industry Center
Guidebook

English

MORE
THAN A
1000
YEARS OLD
PAPER

Hanji
Time-honored
Korean Paper

絹五百
紙千年

KOREAN
TRADITIONAL
PAPER

Hanji

1000

DESIGN—Infusing a sense of flow and lightness into everything from the custom typeface to the banners and wall signage, Studio FNT shed light on the bond between *hanji* and nature. The scripted logo conveys the constant passage of time as well as the craft's ongoing existence.

Hanji

한지문화산업센터
서울 종로구 북촌로 31-9
Hanji Culture and Industry Center
31-9, Bukchon-ro, Jongro-gu,
Seoul, Republic of Korea
E. hanjicenter@kcdf.kr
T. +82-2-741-6600
www.hanji1000.kr

한지에는 닥나무 섬유를 이용해 국내에서 생산한 우리 고유의 종이입니다.
Hanji is a Korean paper produced within Korea using the paper mulberry fiber.

샘플북 목록

1. 고궁한지
2. 대성한지
3. 대승한지마을
4. 덕치전통한지
5. 문경전통한지
6. 성일한지
7. 신풍한지
8. 신현세전통한지
9. 안동한지
10. 용인한지
11. 원주전통한지
12. 원주한지
13. 이상옥전통한지
14. 장지방
15. 전주전통한지원
16. 천양피앤비
17. 천일한지
18. 청송전통한지
19. 청웅전통한지

Sample Book List

1. Gokung Hanji
2. Daeseong Hanji
3. Daeseung Hanji Maeul
4. Deokchi Jeontong Hanji
5. Mungyeong Jeontong Hanji
6. Seongil Hanji
7. Shinpung Hanji
8. Shinhyeonse Jeontong Hanji
9. Andong Hanji
10. Yongin Hanji
11. Wonju Jeontong Hanji
12. Wonju Hanji
13. Leesanguk Jeontong Hanji
14. Jang Ji Bang
15. Jeonju Jeontong Hanji Won
16. Chunyang P&B
17. Cheonil Hanji
18. Cheongsong Jeontong Hanji
19. Cheongung Jeontong Hanji

KCdF 한국공예·디자인문화진흥원
Korea Craft & Design Foundation

* 본 샘플북 표지는 고강한지벽페이퍼의 용융한지 270g/㎡으로 제작되었습니다.

(Left box — partial)

...에서 생산한 우리 고유의 종이입니다.
...n Korea using the paper mulberry fiber.

Sample Book List

1. Gokung Hanji
2. Daeseong Hanji
3. Daeseung Hanji Maeul
4. Deokchi Jeontong Hanji
5. Mungyeong Jeontong Hanji
6. Seongil Hanji
7. Shinpung Hanji
8. Shinhyeonse Jeontong, Hanji
9. Andong Hanji
10. Yongin Hanji
11. Wonju Jeontong Hanji
12. Wonju Hanji
13. Leesangok Jeontong Hanji
14. Jang Ji Bang
15. Jeonju Jeontong Hanji Won
16. Chunyang P&B
17. Cheonil Hanji
18. Cheongsong Jeontong Hanji
19. Cheongung Jeontong Hanji

...문화진흥원
...Foundation

...의 용융한지 270g/㎡으로 제작되었습니다.

(Right box — partial)

Hanji

한지문화산업센터
서울 종로구 북촌로 31-9
Hanji Culture and Industry Center
31-9, Bukchon-ro, Jongro-gu,
Seoul, Republic of Korea
E. hanjicenter@kcdf.kr
T. +82-2-741-6600
www.hanji1000.kr

한지에는 닥나무 섬유를 이용해 국내에서 생산...
Hanji is a Korean paper produced within Korea...

샘플북 목록

1. 고궁한지
2. 대성한지
3. 대승한지마을
4. 덕치전통한지
5. 문경전통한지
6. 성일한지
7. 신풍한지
8. 신현세전통한지
9. 안동한지
10. 용인한지
11. 원주전통한지
12. 원주한지
13. 이상옥전통한지
14. 장지방
15. 전주전통한지원
16. 천양피앤비
17. 천일한지
18. 청송전통한지
19. 청웅전통한지

KCdF 한국공예·디자인문화진...
Korea Craft & Design Foundation

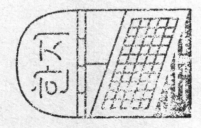

PHYSICAL —The Korean Craft & Design Foundation went to
great lengths to compile a comprehensive study of the 18 remaining
and viable *hanji* makers throughout South Korea.

With this documentation, Studio FNT artfully designed an 18-volume
archive in the form of a boxed set of booklets, complete with unique
emblems like makers' marks.

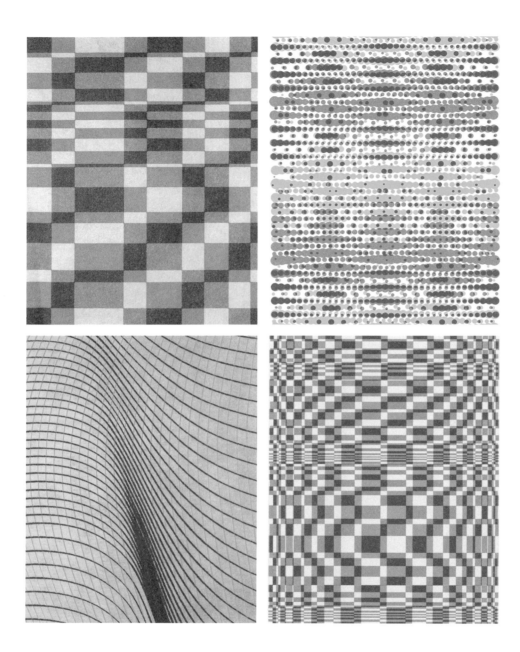

DISCOVERY—Following their work for the Korean Craft & Design
Foundation's Hanji business, and in hopes of actively promoting
the traditional paper, Studio FNT collaborated with Seoul's lifestyle
shop TWL to develop forward-thinking designs, which they applied
to stationery and traditional hand fans.

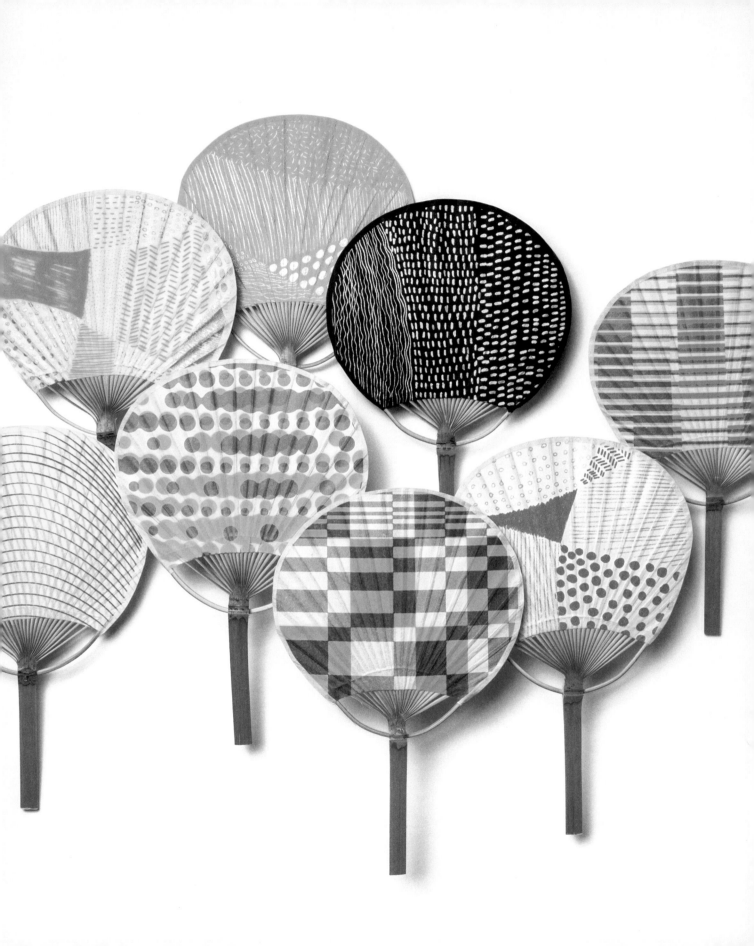

STUDIO   CLIENT   YEAR
STUDIO8585   ONLY WAY IS UP   2023

Studio8585
OWIU

ART DIRECTION   GRAPHIC DESIGN   PRINT PRODUCTION
MARIO DEPICOLZUANE   BENJA PAVLIN   LUNCH PRESS

                          DESIGN ASSISTANCE   TYPOGRAPHY
                          IVA PRIMORAC   ABC ARIZONA BY DINAMO

"We immersed ourselves in the client's universe to try and deeply understand the project at hand," says Mario Depicolzuane. It is that very immersion that led to the long-term partnership with OWIU (The Only Way Is Up). Initially a collaboration on brand identity for the California design and architecture agency's new product line, Studio8585's work evolved into developing OWIU's entire brand universe. As part of this collaboration, Depicolzuane's atelier produced separate yet connected identities for their client's four companies: OWIU Goods, OWIU Design, Inflexion Builds, and OWIU Spaces. "The trust and mutual creative respect that we established early on helped us during the 'not knowing phase' and allowed us to take the extra time we needed for the final form to mature," says Depicolzuane.

Alongside OWIU founders Amanda Gunawan and Joel Wong, Studio8585's head participated in short but intense client workshops to cultivate a close working relationship. The countless references they shared spanned design, architecture, and even gastronomy. For Depicolzuane, a conversation regarding the Danish restaurant group Noma was especially illuminating. There's the main "fine dining restaurant which would be the equivalent of OWIU Design," Depicolzuane recalls, "but they have these other related projects with different branding and wider consumer appeal."

With these concepts in mind, Studio8585 developed an identity that reinterprets the basic elements of architecture—point, line, plane, and volume—through OWIU's four offshoots. The back-and-forth brainstorming that led to these foundational pillars also gave rise to intricate brand assets. For OWIU Goods, Gunawan and Wong wanted packaging that wouldn't immediately be thrown away, nodding to an artisanal Japanese product design approach. Working with the print production consultancy LUNCH, Studio8585 conceived a fully paper-based solution, each box with an outer sleeve that serves as both a protective layer as well as a means of storytelling. The attention to detail—from the white foil-embossed logotype to the Pantone Silver Metallic ink and colored, uncoated paper—makes for a natural expression and a tactile unboxing experience. "The packaging had to reflect the brand ethos and provide the poetic narrative of OWIU's beautifully hand-crafted products," Depicolzuane muses. "It became an artifact in itself, thanks in part to our great synergy."

ONLY WAY IS UP
ONLY WAY IS
ONLY WAY
ONLY

ONLY WAY IS UP
ONLY WAY IS
ONLY WAY
ONLY

ONLY WAY IS UP
ONLY WAY IS
ONLY WAY
ONLY

ONLY WAY IS UP
ONLY WAY IS
ONLY WAY
ONLY

ONLY WAY IS UP
ONLY WAY IS
ONLY WAY
ONLY

ONLY WAY IS UP
ONLY WAY IS
ONLY WAY
ONLY

ONLY WAY IS UP
ONLY WAY IS
ONLY WAY
ONLY

ONLY WAY IS UP
ONLY WAY IS
ONLY WAY
ONLY

ONLY WAY IS UP
ONLY WAY IS
ONLY WAY
ONLY

ONLY WAY IS UP
ONLY WAY IS
ONLY WAY
ONLY

ONLY WAY IS UP
ONLY WAY IS
ONLY WAY
ONLY

ONLY WAY IS UP
ONLY WAY IS
ONLY WAY
ONLY

ONLY WAY IS UP
ONLY WAY IS
ONLY WAY
ONLY

ONLY WAY IS UP
ONLY WAY IS
ONLY WAY
ONLY

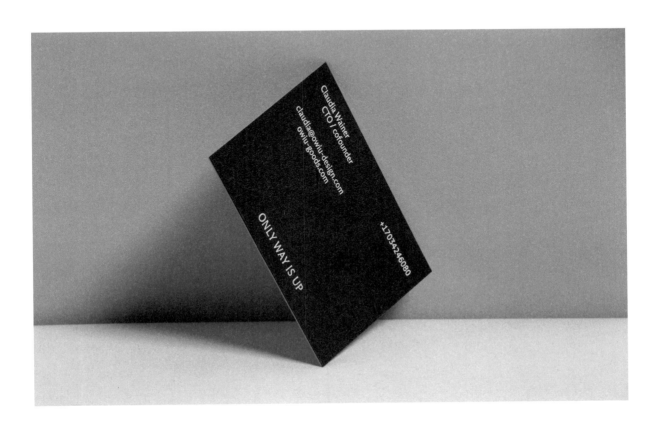

ONLY WAY IS UP

OWIU
GOODS

OWIU
DESIGN

INFLEXION
BUILDS

OWIU
SPACES

WORDMARKS FOR THE FOUR
OWIU OFFSHOOTS

DIGITAL—The markedly expressive ideas of each OWIU sub-brand are reflected in digital spaces through simple motion and parallax features. With OWIU Design, for example, images of different sizes are brought to the top or center, creating the illusion of a line.

INSIDE US WE CARRY INSIDE US THE WONDERS WE SEEK OUTSIDE US WE CARRY

ONLY WAY IS UP
GOODS

With organic layouts and textured paper stock, the packaging and print collateral for OWIU Goods draws from the natural environment.

Addendum

Creative Voyage

Creative Voyage encompasses many things. It is a podcast. It is a publisher and a publication. It is a host to workshops, courses, and events and a maker of thoughtfully produced goods. It is also an intention and a spirit, a process and a platform, a resource and a reimagined way of being. Above all, Creative Voyage is a home for discerning professionals whose practice is their true calling.

As a collective of individuals, we recognize that while our endeavors may be independent in nature, we don't need to traverse this path alone. Along the way, our peers across fields and experience levels—from the novice to the expert—help us to hone our skills, define our values, and better ourselves.

How do we nurture our creative minds and souls? How do we preserve intentionality in an ever-changing world? How do we navigate inevitable obstacles in our inherently intertwined personal and professional lives? At Creative Voyage, we provide the space to connect, to reflect, to learn, and to question. On this long and winding road, we're here to provide the breadcrumbs and sometimes even the entire map. But most of all, we're here to celebrate the journey.

When you enroll in our course on art direction or purchase our latest book, you aren't just opting into an experience or acquiring an object. You are joining a global community. Our co-created organization exists thanks to a wide-ranging network of partners, collaborators, and supporters. Whether you find us on your preferred podcast app, at your favorite bookshop, or on the World Wide Web, our goal remains the same across mediums—to help you, the modern creator, level up and lead a fulfilling, empowered, and inspired life.

Mario Depicolzuane

Molly Mandell
& James Burke

Benja Pavlin

WEBSITE
creative.voyage

CONTACT
hello@creative.voyage

Mario Depicolzuane is a Croatian-born art director, graphic designer, photographer, and publisher. He is the founder of the multidisciplinary design firm Studio8585, and in 2018, he established the Creative Voyage platform. From hosting its podcast to producing the print publication *Creative Voyage Paper* and leading a variety of workshops, he connects fellow creative professionals and encourages them to build rewarding and impactful lives.

Molly Mandell and James Burke comprise the Creative Voyage editorial team, bringing its publications, including the *Creative Voyage Paper,* to life. The duo specializes in creative production and independent publishing consultancy. They are also arts and culture writers and photographers. In addition to authoring their book *Made in Cuba,* they have produced work for the likes of *Wallpaper*, Monocle, Vogue Mexico,* and the *Los Angeles Times*.

Benja Pavlin is a senior designer at Studio8585 and one of the chief design minds behind the Creative Voyage platform. With a background in the humanities, she develops books, exhibition graphics, typefaces, patterns, and printed matter. Her diverse portfolio includes projects with *Outsider Magazine* and the Museum of Architecture and Design Ljubljana, where she helped conceive assets for the Slovenian Pavilion at the 2018 Venice Biennale.

Designing Brands: A Collaborative Approach
to Creating Meaningful Identities

A book by gestalten and Creative Voyage
Edited by Robert Klanten and Mario Depicolzuane

Texts by James Burke and Molly Mandell
Deputy Editors: James Burke and Molly Mandell
Editorial Manager: Lars Pietzschmann

Design, layout, and cover by Studio8585
Typefaces: Signifier & Founders Grotesk by Klim

Printed by Printer Trento s. r. l., Trento
Made in Europe

Published by gestalten, Berlin 2023
ISBN 978-3-96704-122-4
© Die Gestalten Verlag GmbH & Co. KG, Berlin 2023

Bibliographic information published by the Deutsche
Nationalbibliothek. The Deutsche Nationalbibliothek lists
this publication in the Deutsche Nationalbibliografie;
detailed bibliographic data is available online at www.dnb.de

None of the content in this book was published in exchange
for payment by commercial parties or designers; the
inclusion of all work is based solely on its artistic merit.

This book was printed on paper certified
according to the standards of the FSC®.